Praise for *10 Steps to Sales Success*

"I personally recommend Tim's book to anyone who wants to invest and develop their sales confidence. My sales force has read it and is more confident and better equipped to face a very competitive and changing marketplace."

Tom Grande
Western Canada Manager, McCain Foods

"Read this book and stop short-selling your career."

David Chilton
Author, *The Wealthy Barber*

"More than anything, successful sales demands a command and practice of the fundamentals. Tim has written a useful, practical book that delivers the competencies of selling that most anyone could benefit from."

Bob Nelson
Author, *1001 Ways to Reward Employees*

"Tim's book not only teaches, but also inspires. That balance is rare in business reading today. There is something in this book for all of us. It's a must read."

Gary Nason
General Manager Alberta, Norampac Inc.

"I wish I had this resource twenty years ago."

George Fleck
President, EECOL Electric Ltd.

D0951659

10 Steps to Sales Success

The Proven System That Can Shorten the Selling Cycle,

Double Your Close Ratio,

and Significantly Increase Your Income

10 Steps to Sales Success

The Proven System That Can Shorten the Selling Cycle,

Double Your Close Ratio,

and Significantly Increase Your Income

Tim Breithaupt C.G.A.H

AMACOM

American Management Association

New York • Atlanta • Brussels • Buenos Aires • Chicago • London • Mexico City
San Francisco • Shanghai • Tokyo • Toronto • Washington, D.C.

Special discounts on bulk quantities of AMACOM books are available to corpora-
tions, professional associations, and other organizations. For details, contact Special
Sales Department, AMACOM, a division of American Management Association,
1601 Broadway, New York, NY 10019.
Tel.: 212-903-8316. Fax: 212-903-8083.
Web site: www.amacombooks.org

This publication is designed to provide accurate and authoritative
information in regard to the subject matter covered. It is sold with
the understanding that the publisher is not engaged in rendering
legal, accounting, or other professional service. If legal advice or other
expert assistance is required, the services of a competent professional
person should be sought.

Library of Congress Cataloging-in-Publication Data
Breithaupt, Tim.
    10 steps to sales success : the proven system that can
    shorten the selling cycle, double your close ratio, and significantly
    increase your income / Tim Breithaupt.
        p. cm.
    Includes bibliographical references and index.
    ISBN 0-8144-7165-X
    1. Selling. I. Title: Ten steps to sales success. II. Title.

HF5438.25.B726 2003
658.85—dc21   2003007953

This book was originally published in 1999 under the title
Take this job and Love it by Spectrum Training Solutions, Inc.,
Calgary, Alberta, Canada. Grateful acknowledgment is given to
Spectrum Training Solutions for permission to include the illustrations
found throughout this book.

Printing number
10 9 8 7 6 5 4 3 2

To My Parents

Elizabeth and Louis P. Breithaupt,
whom I respect and admire as parents and as friends.
You gave me an invaluable benchmark
of honesty, integrity, and success.
With pride and love I dedicate this book to you both.

I love you.

TABLE OF CONTENTS

PREFACE

Now I know what it's like to give birth, at least in the conceptual sense. Although the gestation period of this book was longer than childbirth, its development parallels the emotions and activities of an expectant mother: mood swings, impatience, anxiety, cravings, anticipation, check-ups, having to choose a name, and the frustration of several missed due dates.

I spent months organizing my thoughts before finally putting ideas on paper and into my tape recorder. When I saw the Table of Contents and the Introduction taking shape, it was like feeling the first kick. I was filled with excitement and an overwhelming sense of trepidation. This could have been my first bout of morning sickness—at least it felt that way. I would wake up thinking, "What did I get myself into? Can I really write a book that salespeople will actually read?"

It appears we've done that. I say "we" because this delivery is the result of a synergistic effort by many individuals. The birth of anything is rarely a solo performance.

10 Steps to Sales Success represents my deepest belief that selling is fun. Selling is one of the most challenging yet rewarding careers in our society. Sales entrepreneurs are emerging as one of the most sophisticated and important players in the business arena. A sales career offers no end of promise, and the excitement of endless possibilities. Selling is a springboard to the fulfilment of all your goals and aspirations. It's my hope that this book will help you and others discover (or perhaps rediscover) the joys of professional selling, and that it will empower you to truly aspire to new levels of success. Life validates that success is a matter of choice, not chance. Enjoy.

ACKNOWLEDGMENTS

The completion of this book has left me with the challenge of expressing my gratitude for the acts of encouragement and support offered by so many people. My indebtedness goes far beyond a thank you. To those who contributed, directly or otherwise, I offer my deepest appreciation.

The following individuals are deserving of a special thank you.

Les Hewitt: My mentor who said, "You need to write a book," and then inspired me to follow through on his idea. Thank you for your undying confidence and support. We just did it!

Shauna Dobrowolski: My executive assistant for over four years—what an outstanding woman. Shauna is the epitome of the human side of business. Her positive attitude is the envy of her peers, and her unwavering support, dedication and enthusiasm formed the cornerstone of this project.

Rod Chapman: My editor who used more red ink than a tax auditor while assuring me it was in the interest of, "stylistic consistency, parallel construction, and a clean manuscript." We are still talking!

Gary Lundgren: His awesome cartoons relate to us all. Thanks for "Bernie."

Special Acknowledgments:

Trish Matthews	Michael Fisher
Anne Milette	David Chilton
Wendy Perry	Ron Cuthbertson
Armchair Critics	Past and Present Customers
Lynn, Stephen, and Michael	

INTRODUCTION: WHY *THIS* BOOK?

As a professional sales trainer, I have discovered a very important aspect of adult learning: people love simplicity. The simpler the better. I wrote this book with that goal in mind; to reveal the simplicity of selling. Selling is simple. Simple is fun. That is why the KISS principle (Keep It Simple Salespeople) prevails. This book offers an approach that strips away the perceived complexities of selling and discusses selling in its purest form: a dialogue between two human beings.

The required skills of an effective sales professional have become increasingly sophisticated. Today's customers are looking for a whole range of products and services to meet their business and personal needs. Customers have become immune to traditional sales techniques. Technological changes, sales automation, deregulation, and the global economy have blurred many product distinctions, at the same time stimulating a highly competitive selling environment. Nowadays, product and price alone will not sustain a competitive edge. We have seen the demise of the "obvious product solution." Your product on its own will no longer stimulate a sale. Your customers can buy virtually the same product at the same price elsewhere, so why should they buy from you? Customers appreciate a salesperson with empathy—the ability to develop a total solution versus simply presenting a product. They also appreciate the efficiency of new technologies, *high tech*, but still want the warmth of the human aspect, *high touch*.

Sales productivity often gets sabotaged by the mechanics of selling. Unfortunately in many cases, selling becomes more of a strategic engagement with the enemy rather than a conversation with a potential ally to your business.

You are about to learn powerful proven techniques of professional selling. As you master the techniques revealed in this book, you too will experience new levels of productivity. Expect your close ratio (successful sales to number of sales calls) to double. No longer will you have to worry about missing your monthly or quarterly sales targets.

If you are like me, the *visual* aspect represents an important part of adult learning. Research suggests that most of the information stored in people's minds enters through their eyes. If your words conflict with your actions, a listener will believe the actions. I have taken my 25 years of practical sales experience and designed a visual representation of what the entire sales process looks like. I am not aware of any other book that presents the entire selling process in visual form.

I write this book with the intent to share my accumulated knowledge and experience, perhaps making your life a little easier. Early in my career I discovered I had a propensity for sales. After graduation from the University of Toronto in 1977, I pursued my love of sales with corporations such as J.M. Schneider, Inc. and Gulf Resources. I then spent eight years in the computer industry with Control Data Corporation, five of them as sales manager.

In 1991, I left the arena to found my own training company, Spectrum Training Solutions Inc. Since then, I have worked with national and international companies and trained thousands of corporate professionals. I describe my style of facilitation as enter*train*ment, because I believe humor contributes significantly to adult learning and retention. I invite you to visit our site at *www.spectrain.com.*

This book introduces you to a tool I use in all of our sales seminars: the Sequential Model of Professional Selling. The Sequential Model has been designed to foster confidence and success through its simplicity while revealing the common denominators of each sales call. Experience has shown that a certain degree of consistency—a common currency—exists throughout every sales call.

This model presents an uncomplicated approach to selling by delivering the core competencies of the entire sales process. The strength of this model lies in the fact that its design and development were guided by input from several resources including my years of on-the-street selling, input from customers, feedback from thousands of sales professionals attending our seminars, and interviews with hundreds of customers. I still sell. Like you, I'm out there every day dealing with the challenges, the frustrations, and the joys of professional selling.

Although each sales call is situational, a logical, sequential series of actions greatly increase the chances of making a sale. This selling process involves the ten steps introduced in Chapter 1. Steps 1 and 2 are important preparatory activities, Steps 3 through 10 are related to interpersonal skills and specific selling skills. All ten steps are discussed in detail throughout the chapters.

The Sequential Model is not a new sales gimmick or another slick technique to trick the customer. Each step of the model, when learned and applied, endows you with the capacity to advance to the next step. It is a proven, field-tested sales strategy endorsed by real-world authorities: my customers.

Of the thousands of sales books available, most focus on limited aspects of selling. Though you can purchase books about specific subject areas such as handling objections, negotiating skills, prospecting, probing skills, closing the sale, and a host of other sales-related topics, very few books present sales as a complete process, from start to finish. I am not suggesting that other sales books are of no value—some are very good. In fact, I periodically refer to other books that I encourage you to read and add to your personal library.

Throughout this book, every aspect of the sales process is discussed in detail, including effective sales negotiation and time management skills. Consider this all-encompassing book as your personal reference, a resource to reinforce existing skills and introduce new skills. As a successful sales professional, you must continually search for any intellectual advantage available. Simply put: to earn more, learn more.

Maximize Your Investment: Six Guidelines

To maximize the concepts of the Sequential Model of Professional Selling, I offer these six guidelines:

1. **Read the entire book.** This is the only way to fully understand the Sequential Model concept. As you progress through the book, ask yourself how you can apply and link each step of the model to your particular sales arena. This book has been written for all sales professionals, regardless of experience. It presents a strategy that can be used by any salesperson to sell anything to any customer.

    In 2000, less than 15% of North Americans bought a self-development book, and less than 10% of those actually read it. Shocking! My guess is that most people who buy a self-help book experience some degree of spiritual or career cleansing. People take satisfaction from the fact they bought it, proudly displaying it on their desk. Their intentions are noble but seldom fulfilled.

You, of course, are different. That's why this book is in your hands. By the way, congratulations on your investment.

2. **Keep the best, toss the rest.** Now just a minute, don't toss this book yet. What I mean is that not all the suggestions and strategies within the Sequential Model will apply to your sales arena. The Sequential Model offers a smorgasbord of ideas and suggestions. Fill your plate with what is appropriate for you. Every industry is unique, so I suggest you examine each step closely and then determine whether to apply it. If you discover just three or four new ideas that enhance your sales confidence, then the investment is worth it. My theory is that we improve and grow one idea at a time.

3. **It may not be your way, but it's a smart way.** The Sequential Model will challenge your thinking and encourage you to reevaluate your current sales approach. Change is difficult. You may need to abandon old habits and embrace new behaviors. Don't be too quick to defend your existing inventory of sales skills. I appreciate that it's difficult to surrender cherished techniques without protest. However, I invite you to reexamine all aspects of your sales habits. My purpose is to stimulate the thinking process, not as an event, but as an ongoing, continuous learning curve. As professionals, we often have to unlearn as much as we learn.

Have you ever stopped to notice how adept our customers are at changing? They jump at the chance for bigger, better, faster, cheaper, and so on. They don't seem to have a problem with it. What's our problem?

I suggest the corporate arena is the catalyst for much of the change we experience. Businesses continually drive change. I am not suggesting a wholesale change to your existing sales strategies, but I'm sure some of your skills could be enhanced or even replaced with smarter skills. Hard work is not nearly as rewarding as smart work. Sell smarter, not harder.

4. **The chapters can be used as individual references.** Although each chapter represents an integral part of the Sequential Model, each can be read as a stand-alone resource. You may find it helpful to refer to one specific chapter and refocus on that particular aspect of selling.

5. **This is not only a book, it is also a resource.** Refer to it often—make it part of your personal development library. Mark it up, highlight relevant sections. It is amazing how quickly we experience intellectual evaporation. Unless new information is reviewed and applied regularly, we revert back to the easy way, our old habits. The goal of training is practice, not competency. Share this little gem with your manager: noone becomes competent by attending one seminar or taking one lesson. Learning is a sequential process, not an event. Selling is like a sport. To become adept at golf, tennis, or any other sport, we must practice, practice, and practice. Only practice makes permanent. There is no other way (if you discover a better way, call me collect).

6. **Make it yours.** Take ownership of the skills you discover in the Sequential Model. Have fun. Simple is fun.

Equity means ownership. You can have financial equity but you also require personal equity in terms of professional, up-to-date selling skills. By reading and applying the strategies in this book, you enhance your intellectual equity and your confidence to sell.

As you work through the book, your enthusiasm for sales will be re-energized. What other profession is financially rewarding, guarantees you a job for life, and gives you the flexibility to establish your own hours? Outside of sports, it is rumored that selling is the highest-paid profession in North America.

Meet My Good Friend "Bernie"

People appreciate good humor and there is no question as to its powerful effect on adult education. Humor is the gateway to learning. I like to think of it as "the lubricant of learning." With that in mind, I introduce you to "Bernie," a rather hapless, sorry-looking chap who will join us throughout the book. Bernie will help us see the humorous side of a profession that can be fraught with highs and lows as we deal with uncertainty and/or stress in a world of rejection.

We can all relate to his frustrations and mishaps as he pursues his sales career and works very hard to please his customers.

Bernie

The Tim Commandments

To encourage the attitude of entrepreneurial selling endorsed throughout the book, I suggest you consider 10 Productivity Questions as you work through the Sequential Model. They are designed to challenge your daily activities and embrace the role of a sales entrepreneur. I refer to these 10 Productivity Questions as the *Tim Commandments.* Consider the *Tim Commandments* as your navigational buoys guiding your activities throughout the day. As you master the Sequential Model strategies, you will develop a new-found sense of confidence and personal satisfaction that will regenerate your enthusiasm for one of the most exciting and rewarding professions, *selling.* The *Tim Commandments* are spread throughout the book to guide you as you complete the steps.

Chapter 1

THE SEQUENTIAL MODEL
OF PROFESSIONAL SELLING

Adult Learning: How It Works

If you haven't read the Introduction, go read it, then come back. I'll wait. The Sequential Model of Professional Selling represents one of the fundamental principles of adult learning: Learning is not an event. It is a sequential process marked by stages of growth and development. Learning is cumulative. As we mature in life, we come to know and accept this principle of continuous process. A child must learn to crawl, sit up, walk, talk—and then to sell. Even superstars like Wayne Gretzky and Tiger Woods had to respect the principle of sequential development. Their parents were instrumental in their success and I'm sure they would be happy to confirm the endless hours of practice required to develop the basics. Attempts to shortcut the principle only result in disappointment, frustration, and a lousy paycheck.

Remember when you were a child wrestling with jigsaw puzzles or building model airplanes and ships? When you finally put the last piece in place, your proudly displayed finished project was most gratifying. During construction, you had to deal with several frustrations: extra pieces, missing pieces, wrong-sized pieces—and the worst part: not realizing you still had glue on your fingers until you rubbed your eye!

The good news is that the Sequential Model of Professional Selling has already been put together for you—no assembly required. It has no missing pieces and comes with an excellent user's manual—this book. The manual represents 30 years of my personal sales experience, learning real-world selling skills on the street. In fact, feedback from my customers helped me write this user's manual. Unlike many other manuals, this one is simple. When you follow the instructions, customers will cast their votes of confidence with orders. A purchase order is the ultimate ballot of confidence. The beauty of this model is that you can always add extra pieces by adding your own unique personality and your own selling skills. You can be the architect of your own personalized selling style using the Sequential Model as your guide.

Although many salespeople constantly search for the secret of "little effort, big returns," or the "quick fix," the selling profession is not immune to the principles of adult learning. There are no shortcuts.

Ten Steps

Guided by the principle of the sequential learning process, I have developed the Sequential Model of Professional Selling. Working with customers coupled with feedback acquired by training thousands of sales professionals has enabled me to create a model that is simple, yet reflects all of the ingredients required to make a sale (Figure 1.1).

The Sequential Model visually presents the ten steps of selling and helps clarify the selling sequence. This is what selling *looks* like. Each step of the model, when learned and applied, endows you with the capacity to advance to the next step. Each step is related to all the others. The final outcome of the sales

The Sequential Model of Professional Selling

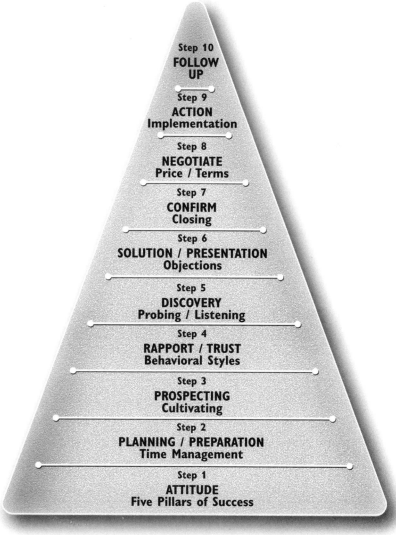

Step 10
FOLLOW UP

Step 9
ACTION
Implementation

Step 8
NEGOTIATE
Price / Terms

Step 7
CONFIRM
Closing

Step 6
SOLUTION / PRESENTATION
Objections

Step 5
DISCOVERY
Probing / Listening

Step 4
RAPPORT / TRUST
Behavioral Styles

Step 3
PROSPECTING
Cultivating

Step 2
PLANNING / PREPARATION
Time Management

Step 1
ATTITUDE
Five Pillars of Success

Figure 1.1

interview is determined not by your ability to perform one step, but by your ability to perform all steps throughout the execution of the sale. Once again, selling today requires a sophisticated set of skills.

Webster's Dictionary defines *model* as: 1) a standard or example for imitation or comparison; 2) a pattern on which something not yet produced will be based. That is exactly my objective: to provide an example, a pattern to be imitated throughout the sales call. The Sequential Model provides the minimum acceptable standards on which to base your performance. Anything less compromises your success. The model gives you the confidence to effectively navigate through the entire sales call. It is a guideline, a blueprint that can be tailored to your specific selling arena.

Don't view the model as a rigid, ten-step strategic engagement with your customer. Each sales call must be situational, guided by the *spirit of the model*. It becomes a seamless interaction with the customer—a very fluid dialogue.

Beginning with Step #1, each step of the model must be successfully completed prior to advancing to the next step. When I say successfully completed, I am referring to success as defined by your customer. To earn the right to advance the sale, the customer must be satisfied with your performance at every step. He or she is the ultimate referee of your performance. Every successfully completed step sets up the next one, steadily moving the potential customer toward a buying decision without pressure. Consider your progress as a series of graduations—complete the required curriculum of each step, graduating to the next one. Bypass a step or leap-frog a step and you seriously jeopardize the end result, which is win–win. Sorry, no shortcuts. No missing pieces allowed.

What Is a Customer? Six Types

To enhance our understanding and comprehension of *customer,* I offer Webster's definition as a logical starting point: 1) a person who buys, especially on a regular basis; 2) a person with whom one must deal. At the end of the day customers are the sole provider of every business—the revenue stream that pays for everything else. You can have the best product, the best accountant, the best management, and so on, but you have nothing without a revenue stream. And the revenue stream is the direct contribution of sales, period. Nothing happens until something is sold.

Let's look at the six types of customers.

1. **External Customer.** These are the people and organizations who have a need for your product or service. They purchase your stuff in exchange for money. They have a budget and will give you some of it in exchange for a solution that meets their needs and expectations. Given that, I affectionately refer to external customers as ones with the *bag of money.* They have the financial autonomy to decide where and how they will spend their budget—the bag of money. The question is, who gets the bag of money, you or your competitor? Who has earned the confidence and trust of the customer? You and your competitor are vying for a piece of their budget—the best solution wins. Know this: Customers vote with their money and complain with their feet.

2. **Allies.** These are the users of your product or service, not the ultimate decision maker. These customers usually don't have a bag of money but they play a vital role in your success. They do not make the final decision but they may have tremendous impact on the outcome. They are often closely connected to the bag of money and positioning them as an

ally to your cause is critical for your success. You must earn their trust and confidence if you expect them to support you at the bag of money level. A caution about allies: They have veto power, the authority to say no. They can give you a hundred no's but can't give you the one yes needed to close the deal. I have seen countless selling hours wasted on allies with the hope of closing the deal. However, allies can be a tremendous wealth of information. Pick their brains and learn how you can differentiate yourself from the competition. Customers buy differences, not similarities. It can sometimes be difficult to ascertain who the bag of money is and who the allies are. Ask questions early in the call to determine who's who in the zoo. Shrink your sales cycle by understanding the players within your accounts. Simply ask them who else may be involved with decisions.

3. **Internal Customer.** These are fellow employees and managers within your place of business. They support you and make you look good to your external customers. Appreciate them and treat them with respect. Unfortunately, they are often the victims of your blamefest: "The jerks in production screwed up again ..." or "The idiots in shipping messed up ..." or "Management gave me a lousy price ..." and so it goes. Poor internal relationships can have fatal consequences for your external customers. I recently saw an anonymous quote that supports my point. "We have less to fear from outside competition than from inside conflict, inefficiencies, discourtesy, and bad service." So true. Take ownership for customer concerns. After all, you are an ambassador for your company, so don't abdicate responsibility for late deliveries, poor service, and inadequate support. Customers really don't care whose fault a problem is or how it happened. Customers aren't interested in fixing the blame.

They want to fix the problem. It's up to you to quarterback all of the company's resources to resolve their problem.

When you work in harmony with your internal customers, external customers become the beneficiary of your internal relationships. In company after company, I see sales working in isolation from other departments. Sales cannot fly solo and expect to service the expectations of external customers. Long-term success means having your entire company and all its resources focus on its customers.

Be aware too of your own personal internal customers, such as family, spouse, and parents. View your kids, spouse, or significant other as your personal internal customers. They also deserve respectful treatment.

4. **Repeat Customer.** They are the jewels of your business. Do the job well the first time and you often get rewarded with another opportunity to serve them. And guess what? They give you more money! You may have heard that it costs up to five times as much to replace a customer as it does to keep one. So, keep them happy. Underpromise and overdeliver.[1]

5. **Born-Again Customer.** These are previous customers who no longer do business with you. For some reason they have forgotten about you or they are still upset with you. I suggest you dig up their file, give them a call, and settle any outstanding grievance. Put your ego aside and offer restitution to satisfy the customer. Do what it takes to resolve the situation. Make amends. Very frequently they will once again be receptive to doing business with you. They often become loyal customers provided you resolve the problem to their satisfaction.

As you work with your customers, you will find the Sequential Model is applicable to all six types. Remember: Pay particular attention to your internal customers.

6. **Bag of Wind.** You guessed it, these people have little or no impact on the decision. They are often an easy point of entry into an account but they seldom contribute to the sales process. In fact they do more harm than good by creating a false sense of authority. There is nothing worse than wasting valuable selling hours on people who cannot help advance the sale. However, I'm not suggesting to ignore these people but rather exploit their knowledge to deepen your understanding and confidence about the account. They may also provide clarity as to who the allies are and who the bag of money is. Knowing these people can prove to be a huge advantage; knowledge is power.

Definition of Selling

The sales profession has offered numerous definitions of selling. With each writer (this one included) comes another definition, another viewpoint. However, see what you think. It's simple. Selling is talking with:

The **right** person at
The **right** time with
The **right** solution for
The **right** price, recognizing
The **right** time to confirm (close).

I call these the five *rights of passage*. Your sales call will only be as effective as the weakest *right*. All five must work in harmony to advance the sale. Imagine the frustration of trying to close the sale by talking to the wrong person at the wrong time with the right solution. Therein lies the challenge of professional selling: earning the right to advance the sale by executing the five rights of passage. You must be in sync with your client throughout the entire Sequential Model or the sale is lost. Worse yet, you may end up forcing the sale and creating buyer's remorse. That's where the sinking feeling of regret creeps into the customer's mind. These five rights give new meaning to "the rights of a customer."

Another definition of selling is, "Selling is the process of disruption." Ultimately, you are there to facilitate change, disrupt your customers' current situation, and improve their business by suggesting they buy from you. Don't expect to walk into a prospect's office and hear him or her say with enthusiasm, "Oh, thank goodness a sales representative showed up! We have done without for so long. We were hoping someone would drop by soon."

It won't happen. If selling were that easy, you'd be earning the minimum wage.

Advanced Selling Skills

By this point, you may have wondered if this book addresses *advanced* selling skills. Legitimate question. Let me answer it this way: I recently worked with a client who was rather insistent on finding an *advanced* selling skills seminar. During our discussion, I suggested that success in a sales call is directly linked to performing the basics well. We have all heard about professional sports teams recovering from a slump by going back to basics. The basics never fail us. Strive for *brilliance at the basics.*

I responded to my client by telling her there is no such thing as an *advanced customer.* In my years of sales experience, I have never heard of anyone referred to as such—tough maybe, but not advanced. I recognize that this is a new concept, but I feel that customers simply represent a variety of positions, some more senior than others. Regardless of their position, all customers have universal agendas, such as "why should I buy from you? . . . how are you going to help my business? . . . what's in it for me?" These questions are common denominators to every sales call. Advanced selling is simply a matter of understanding and applying the Sequential Model, coupled with having a positive attitude and the confidence to pursue a dialogue with fellow human beings, regardless of their position or experience. My client accepted the analogy, and I proceeded to design a sales course using basic sales techniques that met her training objectives.

Consider this: The Carnegie Foundation did a study and discovered that only 20% of a person's sales success comes from product knowledge. It's not just *what* you know about your product but, more importantly, it's *how* you present yourself. This report went on to suggest that up to 80% of success in sales (and life) is determined by a combination of self-management skills and interpersonal skills.[2] Other organizations also support these findings. Think about it. As a consumer, when was the last time you purchased a product from someone you didn't like? Not very often. You probably took your business and your bag of money elsewhere.

In sales, the common denominator, the one universal constant, is people. People need to like you and trust you, and to feel that you respect them, before they buy from you. It makes no difference what product or service you are selling—corporations may "do the deal" but it is *people* who "do the relationship." People buy from people.

Sales Reps Need Not Apply

A question I am often asked is, "What will be the role of the sales representative in the future?" My answer is, "The role of the sales representative as we know it today is disappearing. The underlying shift is from sales representative to sales entrepreneur." The role of a sales professional will not disappear anytime soon, but responsibilities will include a sound knowledge of selling coupled with a professional code of conduct.

Unfortunately, the profession of selling is saddled with a lousy reputation. Rarely do we advertise our careers as, "I'm in sales." It's usually, "I'm in marketing," or "I'm in business development," or "I represent the XYZ company." The actions of one-dimensional sales representatives continue to fuel the less-than-stellar reputation of sales. Most one-dimensional sales representatives are motivated by the one-time hit: get the sale at all costs and take no prisoners. They repeatedly make canned presentations armed with little more than glossy brochures and a box of donuts. Their basic need is survival. Repeat business is not part of their repertoire. The future offers no security for the sales representative.

Businesses are scrambling to differentiate themselves as they compete for a piece of those well-guarded corporate budgets. Sales entrepreneurs are their key to corporate differentiation. The facilitators of corporate differentiation will be sales entrepreneurs, not traditional sales representatives. Customers today no longer tolerate the one-dimensional "sales representative" style of selling.

One of the objectives of this book is to foster a mindset of *entrepreneurial selling.* Your future in selling lies in your willingness and ability to operate more as a business, a mini-enterprise, thinking as the president of ME Inc. Sales organizations are slowly reshaping themselves in an attempt to foster entrepreneurial selling. You are no longer *servicing* a territory but *managing* a business. There is a groundswell of support within the business community supporting the role of the sales entrepreneur.

I am always amazed to see the lack of performance accountability at the sales level as some companies still accept so-so sales results, where performance falls short of revenue targets. With nothing more than a verbal spanking, the representative forges ahead optimistically into next year. In future, sales entrepreneurs will be held closely accountable for all sales-related aspects of their business, including margins, profits, customer satisfaction, expenses, and results.

I fully expect the future will endorse some form of certification or licensing for sales professionals. In fact, the International Standards Organization regulatory body is already looking at it.

The Adult Daycare Center

Entrepreneurial selling also means less time spent in the office. Sales representatives love to hang out at the office. They tend to take refuge in the office, shielding themselves from the hostile sales arena of constant rejection. I refer to an office as an *adult daycare center*. Sales representatives go into the office, play with the other kids, play with the corporate toys, play on the Internet, retrieve e-mail (half of which are junk), swap stories of hardship at the coffee machine, and generally appear to be busy. They are often lulled into sedentary activities, pursuing the art of busyness. Some technologies even encourage the sales representative to hang out at the office—the fax machine is a classic. It's much easier just to fax over information and perhaps place a follow-up call—it will save a trip. In fact upon receiving a request for information, some salespeople will actually send a fax without so much as a follow-up phone call. My preference is to make a face-to-face appointment. If that fails, I will courier a professional, customized package containing the requested information. This method is professional and inexpensive—and courier packages still get attention. Give it a try. If I can't get in to see the person during my initial telephone conversation, I set up a telephone appointment to follow up my package. Don't get trapped in the adult daycare center. Your job is to get out there and sell. You can't hunt from a cave. I recently heard another great line that makes a valid point: "If you want to kill half a day, go into the office for an hour!"

Entrepreneurial selling goes far beyond core selling skills. As long as your customers continue to redefine their expectations, successful selling will depend on developing and managing a more sophisticated set of skills. Consider this: Your goal as a sales entrepreneur is to disrupt current thinking of customers. Challenge established buying patterns and facilitate change by way of relationships, trust, and conversational selling strategies, ultimately satisfying both customer and corporate objectives. In doing this, sales entrepreneurs are guaranteed a job for life, whereas sales representatives are quickly becoming dinosaurs. The sales force of the future will be lean and mean, equipped with an inventory of sophisticated skills, possibly representing a

mini corporate profit center. The future will not be an option for sales representatives. Compensation will be heavily weighted toward performance, and success will be measured by the contribution your profit center delivers to the corporation.

The Sequential Model works only if you work it. Notice it is not available in pill form. There is no easy way, no magic prescription. The model must be applied and worked not once or twice, but during each and every sales call. It is a continuous loop, regardless of the type of customer you are working with. The model is timeless and works regardless of what you are selling or how long your sales cycle is. The ten steps can be compressed and applied in a 30-minute sales call or spread over a sales cycle of one year or longer. Consider this book as your prescription to a healthier, happier career as a sales entrepreneur.

Having just read this chapter some of you may be feeling a little anxious. You have suddenly realized your business card reads *sales representative,* the very title I have unceremoniously denounced. But, don't despair. Don't think that all your customers will hate you and stop buying from you. If they do it's not because of how your business card reads, trust me. My intent is not to discourage you, but rather to nurture an entrepreneurial philosophy. I don't want to read in tomorrow's paper, "Hundreds of distraught sales representatives were seen leaping from tall buildings as sales entrepreneurs looked on." Seriously, my objective is to foster a professional code of conduct guided by the qualities of a sales entrepreneur. You don't have to change your business card, simply change your outlook. Your customers are more concerned with your conduct than what your business card says.

As you work through the ten steps of the Sequential Model, I will continue to refer to both titles, sales representatives and sales entrepreneurs. By now I'm sure you can appreciate that there is a big difference. Sales representatives react, constantly playing catch-up, whereas sales entrepreneurs are proactive, always a step ahead of their customers. Sales professionals can no longer afford to just *represent* the business, they have to be *in* the business. We need to stay abreast of ever-changing customer expectations.

Common currency of a sales call includes trust, rapport, respect, commitment, and knowing that people buy from people. Success today and in the future means recognizing changes within the sales arena. Selling is more sophisticated today than it was even five years ago. Although the core competencies of selling have not changed, change is coming in the form of a longer list of responsibilities. We must manage and embrace change so that it doesn't manage us.

NOTES

1. Cathcart, Jim CPAE. *Relationship Selling: The Key to Getting and Keeping Customers.* Page 100. 1990 Perigee Books.

2. Cathcart, Jim CPAE. *Relationship Selling: The Key to Getting and Keeping Customers.* Page 6. 1990 Perigee Books.

Chapter 2

ATTITUDES OF SUCCESS: FIVE PILLARS

Attitude determines your destiny, quality of life, and sales success. The quality of your attitude affects the quality of your life. These are profound statements but true. The proficiencies of today's sales arena go far beyond selling skills. Attitude is one of these proficiencies. Without it, all other skills are handicapped. *Attitude is what drives the practice of skills.* Attitude has such a compelling influence on selling that this book would be incomplete without a discussion on the five attitudinal characteristics of success. Extensive product knowledge alone affords you little advantage if your attitude is one of indifference or if you lack belief in yourself.

The objectives of this chapter are to share with you the significant role attitude plays in your success and to examine the human aspect of business. This book integrates the human side of business with specifics of professional selling. The two cannot work in isolation. As you develop your sales career, you will be inundated with product knowledge, company policies and procedures, price manuals, and other tools of the trade. People often lose sight of the human side of selling. Why does the sales profession complicate such a fundamental process? We put on our business attire Monday morning, then proceed to divorce ourselves from the human aspect of selling. We become robo-reps guided by a mechanical process. Through a positive attitude, you can refocus and develop a humanized approach with your customers.

A positive attitude will convert an average sales professional into a top performer. It empowers you to achieve new levels of success both personally and professionally. Winners choose to nurture and develop a positive, winning attitude. They understand the importance of a winning edge and use it to differentiate themselves in their own personal life and with their customers. Attitude provides that edge. People prefer to deal with winners.

One of the simplest and best definitions of attitude comes from Elwood Chapman's book, *Life Is an Attitude!* He suggests that, "Attitude is the way you mentally look at the world around you. It is how you view your environment and your future."[1] I agree. Your field of perception and how you view your environment largely determines your attitude. Is the glass half full or half empty? While looking outside, do you see the beautiful view or do you see the dirty window? Is it a partly cloudy day or a partly sunny day? It's up to you. Who wants to do business with a grump? (Maybe other grumps). Be aware that your nonverbal communication sends a very clear message about your attitude. It comes through loud and clear as either negative, indifferent, or positive. Two of these outcomes are bad. You need to believe that what you mentally dwell upon significantly determines your attitude. If you look for the good, you find it: If you look for the negative, there's plenty of that around too. You are what you think.

In examining the traits of top-achieving sales professionals, it becomes evident that it is not their product knowledge and selling abilities alone that set them apart. Their habits and patterns of behavior reflect certain attitudes

One of the challenges associated with maintaining a positive attitude is this little tidbit: Psychologists estimate that up to 77% of what we hear and see throughout our day is negative. We often experience "mental negative drift,"[2] allowing the negative to dominate our thoughts. Take a moment and think about a typical day. How are you feeling by 10PM? It takes conscious effort and energy to remain positive and energized throughout the day. I find it interesting that when asked, "How are things?" or "How are you doing today?" many people respond by saying, "Oh, not too bad." Not too bad? Do you mean that most of the time you are bad, but today you're not *too* bad? Interesting. Tell people you are having a *great* day. It's okay, you're allowed to have a great day. Once again, it's attitude.

Attitudes of Top Achievers

To assist you in responding to the daily challenges of professional selling, let's now examine the key attitudinal characteristics—the five pillars of success—practiced by top achievers. A positive attitude is a prerequisite to applying knowledge. This section will not change things for you, but it introduces you to the person who can.

Attitude #1: Just Did It! Thought into Action

Top achievers understand that life offers choice; you can be an observer throughout your life or you can choose to be a participant. You can choose to live life or choose to merely exist. The choice you make determines whether you live with results or excuses. No one becomes successful by watching someone else perform, although lots of people try.

Many people appreciate the Nike slogan, "Just Do It." It suggests taking action. To me, it smacks of procrastination. "Just Do

It." Yes, but when? Well, soon, someday. Although it can be a good start, "Just Do It" relates more to intentions than to actions. The reality is that too often we judge ourselves by our intentions, whereas others tend to judge us by our actions. The challenge we face as adults is not a deficiency of intentions but a deficiency of action. Intentions are easy. We have lots of them. Sadly, intentions are little more than self-serving feelings of accomplishment. Taking action is the hard part. If we did everything we intended to do we would experience boundless success. Successful people embrace the "Just Did It!" philosophy. They take their thoughts and ideas to the next dimension: action.

People tend to procrastinate. In fact, it is how many of us start our day. We usually swat the snooze button two or three times before we finally drag ourselves out of bed and into work. Adopting the principles throughout the Sequential Model will encourage you to get out of bed because you want to, not because you have a lumpy mattress. The next time you purchase an alarm clock, ask for one without the procrastination option.

Another handicap we face as adults is that we tend to look for the easy way, the path of least resistance. Procrastination becomes our worst enemy, a kind of virus. A dose of positive attitude is the antidote. Life offers another choice; we can choose to experience the *pain of discipline* or the *pain of regret*. The pain of regret is costly and lasts a lifetime, whereas the discomfort of discipline is rewarding and enhances your life. Unfortunately, pain of regret prevails. I shared this theory with my youngest son, Michael. He thought the concept was pretty cool and has since embraced it himself. The discomfort of discipline continues to enrich his life. At 17 years of age, he began taking lessons for his pilot's license. Six months later, I witnessed his first solo flight. A very proud moment indeed. He is always reminding me to exercise the discomfort of discipline.

My eldest son, Stephen, was equally impressed with the "Just Did It!" attitude. Stephen completed the required training to become a member of the Canadian Ski Patrol System. Focusing on his goal, he persevered through two months of first-aid training, passed his ski tests, and became a fully qualified mountain patroller. At age 18, he became the youngest member of the Canadian Ski Patrol System in Alberta. Quite an accomplishment for a teenager. Another proud moment for Dad.

We don't need to look very far to see how society has validated the impact of the "Just Did It!" attitude. Consider Bill Gates. In 1975, he was working in his basement pursuing his love of computers. His mother said it was always a hassle getting him to come up for dinner. At one point, his motivation was probably financial, but not anymore. What keeps him motivated is the love of his work. My father once told me that the true measurement of your love of the job is that you would do it for free. Initially I thought he was nuts but now I couldn't agree more.

Every business today, large or small, was at one point a "Just Do It" idea with an action plan that came to fruition. The company you work at now is the result of someone exercising the "Just Did It!" attitude. In fact, over 50% of the places where we do business didn't exist five years ago. What about the individuals who thought of Trivial Pursuit and Pet Rock, to name a couple? I'm sure they are now basking on a beach while we toil away.

Here are a few suggestions to encourage the "Just Did It!" attitude. Buy yourself a "thought into action" tool. What's that, you ask? A handheld tape recorder (a microcassette)—an excellent tool to have available while you are driving or at home. You think continuously—great ideas or thoughts can pop into your mind anytime, usually when you are driving or caught in traffic. The recorder is very handy and provides the convenience to capture your ideas. My own recorder has proved invaluable. It has been a constant companion to me, especially during the two years I took to write this book. You will find it pays for itself in no time. However, I caution you, be careful where you leave it. My significant other and I were recently on a weekend ski trip. On Saturday morning she had a bit of a smirk on her face. With a degree of hesitation, I inquired as to the look. She told me I had been snoring. As on previous occasions I proclaimed my innocence by insisting, "Yeah, but I don't snore." She just grinned and said, "You know that annoying little tape recorder you're married to?" With great delight she proceeded to play back several minutes of me sounding like a buzz-saw. Busted!

The other "Just Did It!" tactic I use comes courtesy of my father. He would occasionally switch his watch to his other wrist. After noticing this on several occasions, I finally asked him what the heck he was doing. He told me that because it feels so awkward on the other wrist, it was a great way to remind himself to do something. Go ahead, switch your watch, or even a ring. It does feel awkward. Next time you get an idea or think of a must-do item, switch your watch or ring. (Tying string on your finger would look silly.) You can switch it back only after you have taken action on your idea. It works for me.

Attitude #2: Set Goals—Daily Destinations

The second attitudinal characteristic found among top achievers is that they set goals. They take advantage of the numerous benefits goal-setting offers. Most of us view goal-setting as a laborious exercise fraught with uncertainty. Did you know that only 5% of North Americans are committed to written goals?[3] I'm not talking about writing a to-do list scribbled on a Post-It-Note or a napkin. I mean a clear, concisely written goal. The to-do list simply represents a shopping list of activities, chores to be performed throughout your day. As a sales entrepreneur, you must get into the mental habit of thinking in terms of end results rather than being satisfied with "busywork."

There is a parade of excuses as to why people do not set goals. The most common one is, "They don't work," or even worse, "How do I know what I'll be doing in five years?" Instead of creating our future, we have been conditioned to react to the present. Too many people today seek the quick fix, hoping for some *rescue fantasy* to magically appear and salvage them from their boring life of routine and occasional luck.

In fairness to the goal-setting exercise, recognize there are two sides to every story. On the lighter side, I offer you the top ten reasons why you may choose *not* to set goals.

Reasons Not to Set Goals

1. No forward thinking is required.

2. You will always be successful—no accountability, no disappointments.

3. Your week is already full. Maybe you'll set goals next week.

4. You have already reached your destination. Life has little more to offer.

5. It gives you a good reason to keep buying lottery tickets.

6. You can hang out with other aimless drifters. Like-minded people love company.

7. The 95% of North Americans who don't set goals can't be wrong. They may be mediocre or very average, but not wrong.

8. You'd rather live by other people's goals. It's easier if they set them.

9. No goals = no failure.

10. To-do lists work just fine for me.

Now, of course I am being silly, but these reasons to not set goals are scarier than you think. I certainly hope you didn't highlight any of them. Unfortunately, many people do buy into this mentality.

Goals offer a host of benefits and the one that impresses me the most is that goals provide a destination. How do you know where you are going in life if you don't have a destination? Most of us spend more time planning our weekend, holiday, or party than we do our own lives. We don't plan to fail, we fail to plan. You have probably heard or read these ideas many times before. That's because they are true. Once again the path of least resistance and the pain of regret prevails.

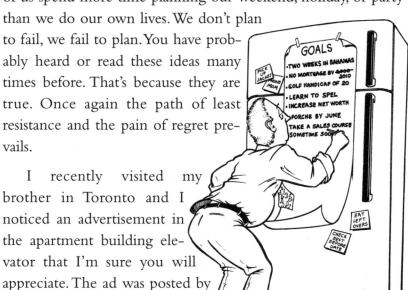

I recently visited my brother in Toronto and I noticed an advertisement in the apartment building elevator that I'm sure you will appreciate. The ad was posted by a financial services company and in bold print asked the question, "Where will you be in five years?" It then offered four choices: (a) Driving a new car? (b) On a vacation? (c) In a new home? (d) In this elevator? I cracked up. Not only was the ad amusing, it delivered a powerful message. Unfortunately, given that only 5% of us have written goals, financial or otherwise, I'm sure "d" is the answer in most cases.

How To Set SMART Goals

With an eye to simplicity, I offer the SMART approach to developing your goals.[4] Don't let the apparent simplicity of the SMART theory prevent you from using it. It works. Just ask your mentor or anyone you know who is experiencing success. By the way, if you don't have a mentor, get one.

The **SMART** Approach:

> Specific (dates, numbers, times, etc.)
> Measurable (end result)
> Attainable (to me)
> Relevant (to me)
> Trackable (progress of goal)[4]

All five criteria must be in place in order to achieve your goal. Don't be overzealous. Be realistic and set goals that are relevant to your environment and to your future. Don't be guided or influenced by the goals of other people such as family, friends, managers, or coworkers. The SMART approach to goal-setting provides a way to articulate what you need to accomplish and where you are going.

The following example illustrates the simplicity of a SMART goal: I will save $500 by December 20, starting June 1. This goal satisfies the SMART criteria, including when it starts. Note that I didn't state, "I want some extra cash for Christmas."

I stated a very specific goal, a SMART goal. Now I have a destination. My next step is to set short-term goals to ensure I reach my destination of $500 by December 20.

Goal-setting is most effective when goals can be accomplished within a reasonable period of time. Many people associate goals with a large window of time, five to ten years into the future, but goals are not reserved for long-term thinking only. Long-term goals are only achieved by setting daily, weekly, or monthly short-term goals. Few people appreciate that goals can become a daily exercise. What's my goal for today? You must think of daily or weekly goals as stepping stones that eventually lead to your longer-term goals. Perhaps Charles Noble said it best, "You must have long-range goals to keep you from being frustrated by short-range failures." The feeling of accomplishment is highly rewarding. This feeling fuels your motivation to remain focused on your short-term goals, en route to your ultimate long-term goals. Without goals, we periodically experience *accidental success*. It's called a fluke. Consider a professional sports team. A hockey team doesn't win the Stanley Cup by winning one or two games. Victory stems from a series of wins during the season and post-season, one game at a time.

Valuable Benefits of Setting Goals

There are several important benefits of goal-setting. The process:

- sets a destination, daily or otherwise
- clarifies purpose
- motivates you to action
- delivers a sense of accomplishment
- provides a benchmark of success
- validates that you are successful
- builds self-esteem
- provides a clear commitment

The SMART process stimulates a clear commitment from you to achieve your personal and professional goals. Commitment casts aside self-imposed barriers such as procrastination, the virus I spoke of earlier. Consider this story taken from Lee Boyan's book, *Successful Cold Call Selling:*

> Well, most people feel safer in a twin-engine plane. They figure if one engine quits, you have another one to keep you up. But consider this. It takes a lot more pilot skill to keep a twin-engine aircraft flying with one engine out. It's terribly unbalanced. It's especially tough in bad weather. Worse, if you have to make a forced landing in bad weather.
>
> But pilot skill is only part of it. The real reason you may want to consider a single-engine airplane safer is this. If that engine quits, the pilot is totally committed to land that bird. There is no other option. Total attention, skill, and effort are concentrated on bringing it down as gently as possible. No distractions.
>
> A twin-engine pilot, no matter how skilled, isn't applying all of that skill to the one critically important task. A twin-engine pilot's mind is going back and forth struggling with a dilemma. Should I keep it up? Should I bring it down?[5]

I am sure many people drift through life like that. They never fully commit to a specific goal. They dabble in this and that, not doing anything very well. Don't simply *try* something, commit to it. Success requires unshakeable commitment: Commit your full attention, your energies, and your skills to fulfill your goals. If you only *try* something, it becomes a very trying experience. Be passionate, not merely interested. Don't be like the kamikaze pilot who flew 17 missions. Get focused.

I recently set a personal SMART goal to lose 15 pounds within 90 days. The goal kept me focused, kept me on course and ensured that I did what was necessary. Goals keep you focused regardless of whether you like the necessary activities. I didn't particularly cherish the thought of dining exclusively on cabbage soup and veggies, but those activities were necessary. The discomfort of discipline.

Tim Commandment #1
Set personal and professional SMART goals frequently.
Ask: What are my personal and professional SMART goals for today, for this week?

Dynamics of Motivation

To further stimulate you toward action, let me share some thoughts on motivation. Much has been written on the subject of motivation. Sales managers are always searching for the elusive magic formula to get their representatives fired up and motivated. But only you can motivate yourself, no one else can. Motivation must come from within. Your manager or spouse may be able to light a fire under you, but only you can light a fire *within*.

Motivation is understanding and appreciating the dynamic relationship between career goals and personal goals. Many people feel that our personal goals are the most important aspect of motivation. I challenge that. It is through the success of our career goals that we are able to pursue our personal goals. It's called a paycheck. How else, except for winning a lottery or receiving an inheritance, can we realize our personal goals? If we view our careers as a vehicle to achieve our personal goals, then we are motivated. If not, then we are saddled with the, "I have to go to work" attitude versus, "I *choose* to go to work." In terms of personal goals, I'm not suggesting money is our ultimate goal but money does allow us to pursue what makes us happy. Let's face it, money is important. In fact, I put it right up there with oxygen. (Another upside to money is it keeps the kids in touch.)

Life only rewards players, not spectators. There is no admission charge for players, but there is always a charge for spectators. The spectators of life pay a high price for their admission and don't even realize it. Life is not a spectator sport. If you are not motivated by your career, then get one where you are.

Motivation has two faces. We can be motivated *away* from something such as a bad job or bad manager (negative stress); or motivated *toward* something such as a promotion or a new career (positive stress). As Abraham Maslow theorized, we all live guided by a hierarchy of needs. Once lower-level needs such as food and shelter are satisfied, a person moves up to higher-level needs, such as esteem and friendship. However, Maslow also tells us that satisfied needs do not necessarily motivate us to move up to higher-level needs. We become content with what I call the FDH syndrome: fat, dumb, and happy. Satisfied needs do not motivate. We must take responsibility for ourselves and set SMART goals to stimulate motivation. Accomplishments and achievements are more satisfying than living with routine and monotony.

Attitude #3:
Self-Esteem: Sell Yourself to Yourself

Libraries offer a host of publications on self-esteem, all offering various definitions. In the interest of clarification, I offer you my definition: "Self-esteem is the conscious appreciation of our own worth and importance, the reputation we have with ourselves. It is an attitude of acceptance versus envy." Accept who you are and what you have rather than what you don't have. Learn to be happy with what you have while you pursue what makes you truly happy.

Self-esteem not only empowers you to *feel* better about yourself but it allows you to *live* better. The level of your self-esteem has profound consequences for every aspect of your performance and your existence. Without question, self-esteem is the most important of the five attitudes. Self-esteem goes far beyond that innate sense of self-worth that presumably is your human birthright. It is about confidence in yourself, confidence in your ability to think, confidence in your ability to cope with life, and the confidence to recognize your right to be successful and happy. To trust your mind and to know that you are worthy of success and happiness is the essence of self-esteem. When you trust your mind, you reinforce your worth and you will more likely persist in the face of difficulties and daily challenges. Research suggests that individuals with high self-esteem persist at a task significantly longer than individuals with low self-esteem. This reinforces trust in your mind. If you distrust your mind, you are more likely to be mentally passive, to bring less awareness than you need to your activities and to be less persistent in the face of difficulty.

Personal Self-Esteem and Career Esteem

Esteem includes not only your personal self-esteem but your career esteem as well. Career esteem is how you feel about your job, your company, your boss, your product, or your service. Are you committed to the career aspects of esteem? If not, you will probably want to take your job and shove it. Your career attitude will come through loud and clear to your internal and external customers.

If you are not happy with the career aspects of your life, consider finding another job. Get paid for what you love to do. When you enjoy your job everyone benefits, at work and at home.

Success is often jeopardized by the self-imposed limitations of low self-esteem. Many of us are our own worst enemies. Perhaps the greatest liability sales representatives have is low self-esteem. They often pursue sales careers handicapped by low self-images. Low self-image and low self-esteem are further fuelled by the fact that sales professionals live in a world of constant rejection. We are too hard on ourselves even before things go wrong. Often negative self-talk—the conversation within our mind—supports a predetermined outcome: "I can't do that . . . I'll probably screw up . . . I won't be successful." And so it goes. It becomes a self-fulfilling prophecy. I once heard personal and professional development expert Brian Tracy say, "We shoot ourselves in the foot and then admire our marksmanship."[6] You must learn to appreciate your own worth and importance. (We'll get to how you can do that in a minute.) "Healthy self-esteem corresponds to rationality, flexibility, admitting mistakes, creativity, and a receptiveness to change. Poor self-esteem corresponds to rigidity, blindness to reality, resistance to change, and limited productivity."[7] Where do you fit in?

Top-achieving sales professionals have a high regard for self. They believe in themselves and understand that you only sell as well as you feel. When we feel good about ourselves, our ability to be effective with our customers is enhanced. However, feelings are not facts. Just because you may *feel* incompetent doesn't mean that you *are* incompetent. Sometimes you may feel that you are not performing up to your usual standard but in fact you may well be. By trusting your decisions and your judgment, you enhance your sensitivity to your customers' needs. Your own insecurities may prevent you from focusing on your customer. Without high self-esteem we live in a house of cards, built on a weak foundation.

Three Ways to Build Self-Esteem

To fuel your self-esteem, I offer three suggestions.

1. Creative Visualization. Use mental imagery to see yourself successfully engaged in sales situations or personal situations, embracing new behaviors. When you see yourself actually acting or thinking in a new way, you begin to let go of old programming. A new reality starts to take shape. For your reality to change, you must picture and accept yourself taking on the new behavior. Some mental preparation is required prior to thinking positively. The goal of visualization is to make the mental practice similar to the physical practice. We must *think positively* before we can *act positively*.

Visualization means "seeing success before it happens." See yourself on the podium prior to the event. By visualizing success, top achievers actually increase the chances of it happening. We move toward what we picture in our minds. A flushing of negative, self-defeating thoughts must occur before the mind can receive and act on new images of success. Athletes have been using the advantages of visualization for decades. They visualize the end result prior to the event itself. They develop a mental blueprint to get a clear image of what needs to be done. In his book, *Advanced Selling Strategies,* Brian Tracy talks about the value of a "mental rehearsal" prior to the sales call. He suggests that "Top sales athletes can use these same techniques as well to dramatically improve their performance in selling situations."[8]

One of my earlier experiences with creative visualization was when I was teaching my daughter, Lynn, how to water ski on one ski. Her earlier slalom attempts had met with frustration and disappointment. She had fallen several times. (Not to mention that the gas gauge in the boat was falling as well.) We took a break and sat down on the dock and I asked her to close her eyes. I then walked her through a mental picture of success where she could see herself up on one ski. I had her confirm aloud what she saw and how she felt about it. Well, you guessed it. On her very next attempt, she got up on one ski. It worked! We were both elated. In fact, she almost fell again as she was filled with excitement and momentarily forgot what she was doing. As Lynn and countless others have discovered, creative visualization elevates your readiness to perform. Give yourself a competitive advantage.

2. **Balance.** A balanced life is another way to foster self-esteem. Goals should not just be set in the area of business. No one has ever said on his or her deathbed, "I wish I had spent more time at the office." Top achievers set goals for all aspects of life. If not, they get out of balance and forget about other dimensions in their lives. The six components of a balanced life are family, health, work, spiritual, intellectual, and social. Examine each one and make time for the things and people that really count in your life. Successful people have come to appreciate the big picture and make a conscious commitment to personal development. They have learned that becoming a well-rounded person has as much to do with pursuits outside the office as with professional development. Success means having "passion pursuits" such as hobbies, personal interests, sports, or other extracurricular activities outside of work. These make for a well-rounded

salesperson who doesn't live life as a couch potato, a mouse potato, or a spectator, but as a participant.

The downside is that without a balanced life, we fall into an activity trap, constantly on the go. We lose our perspective, our energy, and our sense of humor. Life is not that serious; let's take humor more seriously. Humor prevents hardening of the attitudes. Consider the mantra: Think fast, live slow.

Work complements your financial goals. To develop your financial goals I suggest you read David Chilton's book, *The Wealthy Barber*. He delivers excellent strategies to achieve your financial goals, all the while endorsing the KISS principle. David's book will also help you get out of financial quicksand. I'm sure everyone with maxed-out credit cards can relate, they spend themselves to wealth.

3. Read, Read, Read. My final suggestion for maintaining high self-esteem is to read, read, read. Read other resources and materials, listen to audiotapes, attend seminars, and learn from successful people. *You simply do not have enough time in life to make all the mistakes yourself.* Learn from observing others. Don't go through life learning and training by trial and error. It's too expensive. As a friend once said to me, "Do as I say, not as I did." Consider this: if you think professional training is expensive, try ignorance. We cannot learn in isolation. The more intellectual inventory you acquire, the more resources you can draw on, and the better you will deal with daily challenges and stress. Strive to become mentally fit by feeding your mind with highly nutritious mental foods. Feed it mental protein instead of mental junk food like mindless television shows and radio gibberish. The average North American spends upwards of 22 hours a week in front of the television and 5-10 hours on the Internet. It wouldn't take that many hours with a good book to distance oneself from the pack. Many adults continue to live on a diet of mental pabulum, only digesting what is absolutely necessary, nothing more. What you take in today transcends into the person you become tomorrow.

Build your personal development library at a rate of one new book every month. I suggest you start by reading Dale Carnegie's classic, *How to Win Friends & Influence People*. It's a "must read" for people in all walks of life. To earn more, learn more.

Two Types of Knowledge

Every day we are bombarded with new information, new technologies, and new and improved products, all representing new knowledge. But in fact, where we are today, technologically, is comparable to where the aviation industry was in 1950. We ain't seen nothin' yet. I like the statement from author Warren Bennis: "The factory of the future will have only two employees, a man and a dog. The man will be there to feed the dog. The dog will be there to keep the man from touching the equipment." Again we must unlearn as much as we learn. One of the greatest gifts you can give yourself is to learn how to learn.

My theory is that there are two types of knowledge: core knowledge and peripheral knowledge. During our lifetime, we acquire core knowledge (math, science, language skills) which remains constant throughout the centuries (eg., 2 + 2 = 4, and will never change). Peripheral knowledge is the stuff we learn that reflects current technologies and current philosophies. Peripheral knowledge is perishable; it comes and goes. We appreciate that it may very well be obsolete in ten years. Newly acquired peripheral knowledge should come with a "best before" date stamped on it: "For best freshness, utilize this knowledge before the year 2010." Just as we clean out our refrigerators, we need to purge our minds once in a while. An example of peripheral knowledge is keyboarding, a skill currently taught in high schools. Keyboarding is a classic example of peripheral knowledge that is already becoming obsolete. Keyboards are being replaced with voice recognition and voice-activated computers already on the market. Many products we enjoy today are vulnerable to technological obsolescence as the lifespan of products continues to shrink at an alarming rate.

A combination of core knowledge and peripheral knowledge is the key to personal and corporate survival. As I mentioned earlier, the competitive arena demands acquisition of knowledge, and constant investment in career development. We must continually search for any intellectual advantage available. The acquisition of new knowledge fuels self-esteem. However, I caution you, knowing is different than applied knowledge. In Napoleon Hill's book, *Think and Grow Rich,* he makes a good point: "Knowledge is only *potential* power. It becomes power only when, and if, it is organized into definite plans of action and directed to a definite end."[9] One of my national accounts, Dun & Bradstreet, has a great expression: "Knowledge allows you to play, applied knowledge allows you to win."

Stay in school by becoming a lifelong student of your profession. Unquestionably, knowledge is the currency of the future, and today's world takes little pity on those who remain lazy about learning. Lifelong learning is a form of personal insurance. Protect your future.

Attitude #4: Comfort Zone—Stretch It

As two caterpillars were returning from a day of fun in the sun, they noticed a beautiful butterfly overhead. One caterpillar looked at his friend and said, "Gosh, look at that. You'd never get me up there."

This classic comfort-zone syndrome is familiar to most of us. We go through life living within our limited range of experiences, our comfort zone, hesitant to explore new experiences and venture into the discomfort zone. The *discomfort zone* is unfamiliar territory outside of our existing inventory of experiences. A comfort zone includes life experiences that feel natural, safe, and normal to us. Been there, done that, got the T-shirt.

To further our understanding of the comfort zone we must discuss our subconscious minds. No doubt you have some awareness of the workings of your subconscious, as hundreds of books discuss the subject. My interpretation of the subconscious mind is that it represents an inventory of all our life experiences, a warehouse full of perceptions, beliefs, and self-images. Our subconscious mind is our comfort zone.

All our conscious thoughts and daily experiences, positive or negative, contribute to the building of our subconscious mind. Our subconscious mind thinks in pictures. We become what we see. If we think failure, we get it. If we think success, we enhance our chances of achieving it. Henry Ford said it best, "Whether you think you can or can't, you are probably right." Our subconscious mind's impact on our behavior is so all-embracing that it becomes the single biggest barrier to growth, to stretching. Our subconscious rules! We minimize stress and anxiety when we act within what is appropriate to our subconscious. If we see ourselves as losers, then we are. But as Zig Ziglar says, "Failure is an event, not a person." Remember that.

Most of us are risk averse—we are constantly searching for security, content to live within our established comfort zones. These life experiences or behaviors have been repeated for a long time; we take comfort in the predictability of the outcome. We respond within our established repertoire of behaviors—our comfort zone. Stretching our comfort zone involves embracing a totally new activity, something never before experienced: bungy jumping, skydiving or, for some of us, making cold calls! It must be a totally new adventure, never before experienced, to qualify as a stretch. I'm not talking about going to a new restaurant—that doesn't cut it as a stretch. As the saying goes, even a turtle has to stretch it's neck out to get ahead.

Venture into the Discomfort Zone

Top achievers realize that growth comes only by setting goals that require them to stretch their comfort zone. Yes, stretching adds an element of risk. It seems a lot of people don't understand that the rewards come after the risk, not the other way around. To experience the rewards of life, we must pay up front. Interestingly enough, we never know when we will be rewarded, but the rewards do come. Those who don't invest up front always search for the easy way, convinced that it exists. Don't go through life picking only the low-hanging fruit.

As children we are always exploring, taking risks and trying new adventures. Unfortunately as we age, we become more rigid in sticking within our comfort zone. If we inadvertently venture into the discomfort zone, or we are forced into it, we immediately attempt to recoil back into our comfort zone. We cocoon ourselves in our comfort zone, protecting ourselves against possible failure or embarrassment.

Successful sales entrepreneurs are not necessarily more competent, but they do look for ways to grow and stretch. They willingly expose themselves to new things by venturing into the discomfort zone. Use your comfort zone to rest in, not to live in. Use it to consciously relax and reenergize as you visualize performing your next challenge.

Take a piece of paper or even at the bottom of this page write down the last time you willingly experienced a stretch. Give it some thought. Drawing a blank? Don't feel bad, most people do. Note that I said willingly, not accidentally. On a personal note, I would like to share a story where I stretched my comfort zone. I went skydiving. I climbed to 11,000 feet and jumped out. It was a tandem jump where the jump master was strapped onto my back and he had the parachute. The two things I liked best about my tandem jump were freefalling for a full 60 seconds at 125 mph—wow! and the jump master assuring me he was anxious for a successful jump as well. You see, sometimes life itself presents us with challenges that take us out of our comfort zone, forcing us to experience new things. It may be a spouse, parents, boss, or sales manager forcing us to stretch. Don't be like our caterpillar friends and wait around to experience a forced stretch. With that thought let me ask you two provocative questions;

1. When was the last time you did a first time?

2. How old are your stories? (Ouch!)

You may not like the answers but your customers expect you to be interesting as well as interested. Venture out and get some new material.

Tim Commandment #2
Use visualization and SMART goals to stretch yourself. Ask: What is/was my stretch for the month?

How To Stretch: Two Methods

I offer two strategies on how to stretch your comfort zone. Some stretches are planned, others are spontaneous (unplanned/impromptu).

1. **Planned.** Plan to engage in a new activity. "I will set a goal to do X by the end of the week." This gives you time to prepare and visualize your success.

2. **Spontaneous.** See an opportunity and go for it. Don't wait around thinking about it or hoping it will come back another day.

I like to be spontaneous, although I did plan the skydiving. I "Just Did It!" Another suggestion is to experience mini-stretches to start, slowly building your confidence to stretch. Don't feel you have to jump out of an airplane tomorrow.

Let me share another real-world example of how the "Just Did It!" attitude coupled with SMART goals worked in harmony to achieve the desired result of stretching the comfort zone. While facilitating a customer service seminar, I used the example of bungy cord jumping as a classic comfort-zone stretch and asked if anyone had experienced it. The only response was from Lawrence, aka "Slim." He said he intended to do it but was too broke (using the financial angle to procrastinate). A bungy jumping facility was available only minutes away. My cofacilitator agreed it would be appropriate to take Slim and the group on a little field trip. The rest of the group and I kicked in the cash required for Slim to make the jump.

Slim jumped willingly. He "Just Did It!" It was great to watch discomfort of discipline in action. Within two hours of Slim's mentioning he wanted to do it we removed the barrier and he did it. We returned to the seminar and of course Slim didn't learn a darn thing the rest of the day. He was bug-eyed and as high as a kite, intoxicated by his new experience. He got the T-shirt (and the video). He couldn't wait to share his new experience with his wife and friends. He was so proud to say, "I Just Did It!" The same type of opportunities are open to you.

What makes experiencing a stretch so attractive is that my informal research suggests that approximately 90% of the time people respond to their new experience by saying, "Wow, that was great. I'd do it again." Most people do it again because the next time is simply repetition, replacing the initial fear with enjoyment. What Slim and countless others have learned is this: Fear dissolves by way of participation. There is no other way. Nonparticipants live with fear, anxiety, stress, and well-rehearsed excuses. This baggage spills into your career, eroding your enthusiasm, your drive, and your commitment. There are no limitations to the frequency of stretching and experiencing new things. All you need is permission from yourself. My next personal comfort-zone goal is scuba diving. I don't feel particularly comfortable under water but it's something I plan to pursue. My son Stephen is a certified scuba diver and he tells me, "It's awesome." After all I have a 90% chance of enjoying it.

Attitude #5: Patient Yet Persistent

Patient yet persistent: an oxymoron? Not necessarily. As a sales entrepreneur, one of the biggest obstacles to your success is lack of patience. Statistics suggest that less than 5% of sales are made on the first call and over 80% are made on the fifth call. However, only 10% of sales representatives ever return for the third call.[10] They quit and go back to the adult day care center to hang out with other frustrated sales representatives.

Look around you and you will see mostly quitters. Maybe there is one in your mirror. Consider this: The average person

Ms. Dombrowski, did you get rid of that salesperson yet?

GARRY LUNDGREN/98

who takes up a musical instrument, quits. How many people do you know who play a "little piano" or "a few chords" on the guitar? They tire of it quickly, as results come too slowly. They go on to look for something easier. Likewise, many people who start night school, fitness programs, or sales careers quit. The examples are endless. Many of us are great starters but poor finishers.

This is great news for those of us who truly desire to be successful. It means that if we stick to it, we will be ahead of the pack. Jack H. McQuaig, a pioneering psychologist, claims that the one defining factor of success in sales is persistence. There is lots of room at the top. History is alive with classic examples of persistence. Thank goodness for the likes of Edison (10,000 tries before the light bulb worked), Einstein, Bell, Michelangelo, the Wright Brothers, and Alan Hobson and Jamie Clarke. They never gave up. On May 23, 1997, Alan and Jamie finally reached the top of Mount Everest on their third attempt. Alan said this from the summit, "If there is a lesson in all of this, it is that if we persevere long enough, we can do the dreams."

If you call a potential customer once a year, are you persistent? What about twice a year? Once a quarter, once a month, once a week? Are you persistent? The answer to all of the above is yes. Even by calling once a year you are demonstrating persistence. You are saying to the customer: "I'm still here, I'm not giving up." Harvey MacKay talks about how he has not met a qualified customer he hasn't sold. Some took a while—two to three years—but he sold them. Persistence. When do you give up on potential customers? When they die! Even then, introduce yourself to the new person!

Silver Platter Syndrome

One of the better sales videos I have seen presents the silver platter syndrome. Although the video is probably 20 years old, the message remains powerful. The premise of the silver platter is that the average sales representative gives up after only three or four calls to a potential customer. However, we know that 80% of sales calls are closed after five calls, but only 10% of representatives ever make the third call. The silver platter works like this: You make the first call and the second call, generating some interest from the customer. After the third call the customer may not be sold yet, but is probably interested. You have piqued their interest to maybe 80%. However, having made your two or three calls you give up, moving on to the next potential customer. Once again instant gratification prevails and sabotages the sale. Your competitor shows up shortly after you have abandoned the customer, or you simply gave up. The customer, still at an 80% level of acceptance, now entertains your competitor's proposal. How much selling did your competitor have to do? Only 20%. Gottcha! You just handed that sales opportunity to your competitor on a silver platter. He or she should send you a thank-you note saying, "Thanks for giving up. I only had to do 20% of the sale. Have a nice day."

My question is this: How many potential accounts are you working on where you may be exposed to the silver platter syndrome? Better check it out. How often have you given up on a customer relationship but later discovered that your competitor, who was more persistent, got the sale? It's frustrating and unnecessary. The attitude of persistence will not eliminate the silver platter syndrome but it will certainly help minimize it. Stay focused on the accounts that will truly contribute to your business, even if it takes a year or two to close them.

The problem once again comes back to human frailties. Human beings crave instant gratification and we pursue it with a passion, seducing us away from the task at hand, compromising our focus and deviating our energies. Why take six months to possibly close account X when I can probably close account Y tomorrow?

No one is immune. Our world moves along at breakneck speed as we satisfy our quest for instant gratification. Businesses compete with cutthroat aggressiveness to deliver their products faster, bigger, and better. Heck, even the beer companies responded by introducing the "big mouth" beer can. We can now drink beer 40% faster. We have drive-through coffee, eating, banking, and oil changes. In California, you can experience drive-through marriages and when you die, friends can pay their respects at a drive-through funeral home. Inarguably, the antidote to instant gratification is patience and persistence. We must be persistent to remain competitive but all the while patient enough to work within the customer's timetable. Even in California, "drive-through" customers do not exist—at least not yet.

Sales representatives and customers are often out of sync during the sales process. Sales representatives are guided by their agendas whereas the customers are guided by theirs. Don't let the lure of commissions, bonuses, or quick sales sabotage your patience. Don't close the deal on your timetable in the interest of a fat paycheck. It's all too common for sales representatives to sell what they need to sell versus what the customer needs to buy. This is further fuelled by corporate incentives: "One more sale and I win the TV," or "I might win the parking spot for the month." Sales managers put additional pressure on representatives by demanding they hit month-end or year-end targets. A huge gap is created between the sales representative's selling agenda and the customer's buying agenda.

It Begins with YOU

When you pass away, an autopsy will never reveal your attitudes. They are human qualities that are very personal, very subjective, and controlled entirely by you. Attitude not only determines your final destiny in life, it also determines what kind of journey it will be. The bottom line is that you are where you are in life because of the choices you made. Your job, your income, and your spouse are all a result of *your* choices. The only things you can't change are your parents, siblings, taxes, and death. Take ownership of yourself and start living life to its fullest. We need to stop rehearsing our excuses and accept total responsibility for ourselves. Life sometimes resembles an iceberg: We only realize maybe 20% of our potential and we shortchange ourselves by 80% of a great life. Our life is so abundant with opportunity, we just don't realize it. When we nurture these attitudes within ourselves we naturally increase our capacity for meeting just about any challenge with energy, optimism, and a positive outlook.

It's sad to see the number of people who surrender their lives to mediocrity. I recently read on a flower shop sign, "Treat each day like a gift, that's why it's called the present." It all begins and ends with **YOU**: Your Opportunities are Unlimited.

What I Told My Daughter

When my daughter Lynn turned 18, I wanted to impress her with some fatherly pearls of wisdom, something she would remember and cherish the rest of her life. This is what I told her. "Honey, now that you are an adult, from here on in nobody cares about you." She was crestfallen. She said, "Wow, Dad, that's harsh." My point is this and it applies to all of us: Other than your parents, who really cares about your personal success or hardships in life? Nobody. Who cares if you are the CEO of ME Inc. or picking bottles off the street? Nobody. Yes, your manager has a corporate interest in your performance but if you do not perform, you're fired. Your spouse may love you today but if you do not commit to the relationship, it erodes and you're divorced. Your coach may support you but if you do not contribute to the team, you're traded, and so it goes. Nobody cares other than the few people who may express sadness and sympathy for your plight. It's a rather sobering message to tell a daughter and to share with readers but, unfortunately, life is not very tolerant of those who do not take ownership and responsibility for their decisions. Lynn did not particularly appreciate my little gem of advice, but she understood it. It was a big bite out of the reality sandwich. However, the good news is this: By practising these five attitudes that lead to success, sales entrepreneurs can expand their confidence in their abilities. These high achievers will emanate positive energy and display a high level of commitment to their personal life and to their profession.

The best time to develop a lasting, positive attitude is during the good times. Consciously build on the five attitudinal pillars and use them as a catalyst to heighten your success. Don't find yourself reacting to bad times, struggling to combat low self-esteem or low self-worth. Consider this Chinese proverb: "Dig the well before you get thirsty." Or give this some thought: "The best time to fix a leaky roof is on a sunny day." Something else to consider: If you think you have it tough, spend an afternoon visiting the burn unit or the cancer ward at your local hospital. It's a rather sobering, shocking experience. Trust me, it won't take long before you quickly appreciate how good things really are. Quit taking the good things for granted. Bad times tend to wake us up to the good things we weren't paying attention to.

Your power exists in the now. Harness it and make decisions today that will positively impact your tomorrows.

Congratulations on completing Step #1 of the Sequential Model of Professional Selling. The Attitude Step is your springboard into the other nine steps. However, attitude must prevail throughout the Sequential Model. Attitude is a prerequisite to all other steps. You have now graduated to Step #2, Planning and Preparation.

I close with this quote from George Bernard Shaw:[11]

A master in the art of living knows no sharp distinction between his work and his play, his labour and his leisure, his mind and his body, his education and his recreation. He hardly knows which is which. He simply pursues his vision of excellence through whatever he is doing and leaves others to determine whether he is working or playing. To himself he always seems to be doing both."

NOTES

1. Chapman, Elwood N. *Life is an Attitude! Staying Positive During Tough Times.* Page 5, 1992. Crisp Publication Inc.

2. Chapman, Elwood N. *Life is an Attitude! Staying Positive During Tough Times.* Page 23, 1992. Crisp Publication Inc.

3. Hopkins, Tom. *Low Profile Selling: Act Like a Lamb. Sell Like a Lion.* Page 200, 1994. Tom Hopkins International Inc.

4. Nelson, Bob and Peter Economy. *Managing for Dummies.* Page 124-125, 1996. IDG Books Worldwide Inc.

5. Boyan, Lee. *Successful Cold Call Selling.* Second Edition. Page 37, 1989. Amacom

6. Tracy, Brian. *Winners Seminar.* Calgary, Alberta. 1992.

7. Branden, Nathaniel. *The Six Pillars of Self Esteem.* Page 5, 1994. Bantam Books.

8. Tracy, Brian. *Advanced Selling Strategies: The Proven System of Sales Ideas, Methods, and Techniques Used by Top Salespeople Everywhere.* Page 80, 1995. Simon & Schuster.

9. Hill, Napolean. *Think & Grow Rich.* Page 75-76, 1960. Ballantine Books.

10. Brooks, William T. *Niche Selling: How to Find Your Customer in a Crowded Market.* Page 84-85, 1992. Business One Irwin.

11. Cloke, Kenneth & Joan Goldsmith. *Thank God It's Monday: 14 Values We Need to Humanize the Way We Work.* Page 61, 1997. Irwin Professional Publishing.

Congratulations, you have now completed Step #1

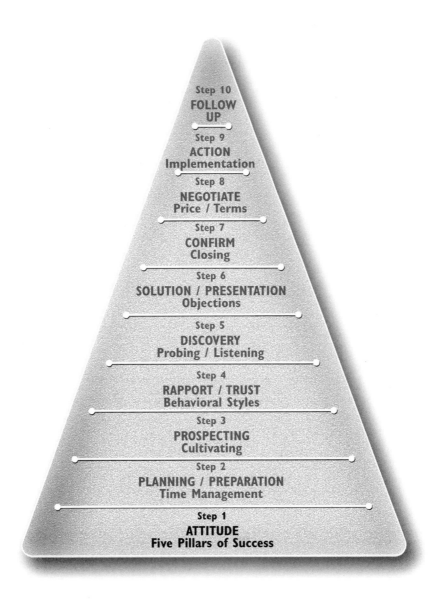

Chapter 3

PLANNING AND PREPARATION: MEASURE TWICE, CUT ONCE

The people at *Training Magazine* tell us that planning will become one of the most important selling tools of the future. Planning is probably the most overlooked selling skill and yet it is the cornerstone to a successful relationship. In proactive selling, salespeople can no longer wing it by developing their plan on the fly. The reality is that very few sales professionals actually commit the time required to thoroughly preplan a sales call. It is far too easy to jump in the car, race over to an appointment, then anxiously await to hear what the first thing out of your mouth will be.

Customers concur that on the top of their list of selling annoyances is a "lack of preparation" by sales representatives. Buyers are most annoyed by sales representatives (notice I refer to sales representatives) who show up at an appointment lacking customer knowledge and saying, "So, what do you guys do here?" or, "Interesting, I didn't know you guys did that." A recent study suggests that 48% of buyers agree that customer knowledge is a powerful selling tool but is underutilized. Planning and customer knowledge working in harmony deliver a tremendous sales advantage. Knowledge is a very powerful differentiator.

It is an accepted truism that humans don't plan to fail, we fail to plan. Why is that? The reason is simple: We are human. By nature, people tend to be lazy,—searching for the path of least resistance, looking for a quick solution. For some reason, many sales representatives think they are immune to any precall planning. Some sales representatives give new meaning to La-Z-Boy. Although most salespeople have a great capability to "improvise," this ability cannot always carry us through a sales call. I suppose part of the reason is that we often see ourselves as being productive simply because we are keeping busy. As long as we are busy we must be doing good things. Wrong. Many salespeople are doers, action people who prefer to start *doing* something instead of wasting idle time planning. They see planning as an activity reserved for engineers, accountants, architects, and so on.

The difference between making or not making a sale depends on several factors, but the amount of homework done by the salesperson is a major contributing factor. The more information he or she obtains prior to the call, the higher the probability of earning the customer's business. Successful entrepreneurs see advance planning as essential to achieving success. Increasing confidence, using time effectively, building credibility, reducing sales cycles, and differentiating themselves from the competition are just a few of the benefits they see. As an investment, planning and preparation increase productivity a minimum of 20%. Think about it. Imagine the outcome of a wedding or a vacation if you didn't take the time to plan or prepare. As one sales manager says, "Even to successfully rob a liquor store, you have to plan." However, be sure that the costs involved in precall planning don't outweigh the potential benefits obtained.

The corporate arena will no longer tolerate selling by the seat-of-the-pants approach. We must plan prior to the sales call. A good carpenter knows all too well: measure twice, cut once.

Imagine the positive results if we did that in our personal lives and in our sales careers. Interesting how there is never enough time to do it right the first time, but there is always enough time to go back and fix it. Winging it is a luxury that sales professionals cannot afford, as it could be months or years before we get a second chance to do it right. A "No Fear" T-shirt said it best, "Second place is the first loser." Unlike the Olympics, the sales arena doesn't offer a silver or bronze medal. Just as an athlete commits to countless hours of training and conditioning prior to a game, a sales entrepreneur must also commit to several hours of preparatory work.

You Have Planned, but Are You Prepared?

History has long confirmed that success is created by proper planning. Imagine a commercial pilot without a flight plan, a builder without blueprints, a coach without a game plan, or a sales entrepreneur without a business plan. Successful sales entrepreneurs plan their work and work their plan. They know the pitfalls of aimless activity, guesswork, or relying on occasional luck.

What's the difference between planning and preparing? I offer you Webster's definitions as well as my own. Webster's suggests that *planning* is: 1) *to formulate a way to achieve or do. Preparing* is: 1) *to produce by combining elements or ingredients; 2) to make or get ready for some purpose.* I augment Webster's definitions by suggesting that *planning* is doing the necessary things to arrive at the appointment ready to do business. Planning includes making the initial appointment, doing your precall homework, knowing your product, developing a sales call objective, and packing your briefcase with the appropriate tools, samples, and order forms. As Webster's says, "Formulate a way to achieve."

Preparation is being in a state of readiness once you arrive. Good preparation ensures that you are ready to perform guided by a sales call objective. Thus, by our definition, planning is stuff we do *prior* to the call and preparation is being ready to perform *at* the call. Customer feedback consistently tells us that sales representatives may have indeed planned, but they are seldom prepared. Once sales representatives have secured an appointment and confirmed the address, they rejoice in a false sense of accomplishment. At best their precall planning is weak and their preparation is nonexistent.

But don't be too quick to view planning and preparation as a laborious exercise. At first glance it may appear to be extra work, but compare it to the consequences of not planning and preparing. The consequences come in the form of longer sales cycles, repeat sales calls, and aimless activity. Good planning does not increase your workload but instead helps you to work more effectively and productively with less physical effort. You may end up with fewer appointments throughout the week, but the time spent planning and preparing will be rewarded with higher close ratios.

Successful entrepreneurial selling demands both planning and preparation. Remember, your Sequential Model allows no missing pieces.

What We Need to Know

The more information we gather prior to the call the better we can plan and prepare for the call. Your product or service may very well help the customer's world move forward, but initially the customer sees you as an intrusion, an interruption. It is even worse if you arrive unprepared and ill-equipped. However, by being prepared and ready to advance the sale, your customer will be flattered by your interest and will begin to relax the barriers and perhaps even entertain your ideas. Advanced planning allows you to differentiate yourself. I am not suggesting that at the planning stage you learn intimate details about your potential customer, but rather that you acquire a conversational understanding of his or her business. Specific details come later. You need to familiarize yourself with the *macro-issues* of the business. Planning is knowing the following pieces of information.

• type of business	*its competition*
• what it does	*private or public company*
• location(s)	*current vendor—how long*
• head office	*political landscape*
• branch offices	*hiring or firing*
• distribution channels	*organizational chart*
• markets	*decision process*
• number of employees	*decision maker*
• how long in business	

I'm sure there are several other issues, but this list certainly guides you in the right direction. Use this as your precall checklist. Customers no longer have the time nor the patience to educate sales representatives.

I have personally experienced the plight of no planning. With hesitation, I share my story. A few years ago I was trying to get an appointment to see Mr. Ray, VP of sales with a large Calgary company. I was selling sales training. Mr. Ray was the decision maker (bag of money) and it took weeks to finally connect with him. My persistence paid off with a 7 AM appointment. I arrived at 6:50 AM planned and prepared, or so I thought. Ten minutes into the call, Mr. Ray looked me straight in the eye and asked, "So, what can you tell me about my company?" I responded with my usual, "That's why I'm here, to learn more about your operation and your specific sales training requirements." Mr. Ray then said, "That's nice, but what can you tell me about my company?" With terrifying speed, I realized my dilemma. I put down my pen and responded with a deafening, "Nothing." Busted! I didn't know a darn thing about his company, didn't even know what they did. What the heck, wasn't it easier to just jump in the car and show up to another sales appointment? Mr. Ray wasn't finished. He knew I was selling sales training so he pondered for a moment (I'm sure it was 20 minutes!) and then asked: "Sales training, eh? Can you teach my representatives to show up unprepared?" I thought I was going to die. I'm not sure what color my face turned, but it was either red, white, or blue. It was 7:15 in the morning and I was experiencing the call from hell. Needless to say, I was utterly embarrassed. Oh, the joys of professional selling. If this situation hasn't happened to you, consider yourself fortunate. The customer hasn't tested you.

This has never happened to me again and it never will. That experience proved to be one of my most valuable lessons of entrepreneurial selling; the value of planning. All I needed to satisfy Mr. Ray's question was this: "Your company is in the business of data management and has been since 1977. Your head office is in Houston and your Canadian office is in Calgary with approximately 40 employees." I'm sure Mr. Ray would have been satisfied with my conversational knowledge of his business and the call would have proceeded. I would have earned the right to continue.

By the way, after about 30 minutes with me doing the backstroke in Mr. Ray's office, he finally agreed to evaluate our seminars by attending himself. We eventually did business.

I want to make it clear at this stage that we are not out to identify our customers' specific needs and requirements or identify how we can help them out. We can't possibly learn their specific needs until we meet them face-to-face and conduct a needs analysis by asking a series of probes. Annual reports and company brochures do not reveal customer needs. Only customers themselves can reveal their specific needs. Our precall planning is done to reveal only the macro-issues of their business. Face-to-face dialogue with the customer is the only means available to reveal the micro-issues, such as specific requirements, nuances, ,and particular needs.

Where to Find It

We live in the information age, where knowledge abounds. The amount of information we are bombarded with can be rather daunting—we are exposed to over 1,000 pieces of information a day, most of it useless. As a sales entrepreneur, we cannot afford to be wading through reams of useless information. We need to identify and peruse sources of information that will deliver reliable, informative, intelligence about our customer. These sources include:

- the internet
- annual reports
- Dun & Bradstreet
- trade journals
- the company receptionist
- old files
- newspapers
- information brokers
- business library
- brochures/catalogs
- company newsletters
- industry associations
- other sales entrepreneurs
- friends in low places
- their sales department

I am sure your experience will offer other avenues to gather company intelligence. One of the best ways to gather intelligence quickly is to call the company and ask to speak directly to one of their sales entrepreneurs. Introduce yourself, tell them that you are doing some homework, and ask for their help. This is a great source of rich information, often overlooked, and my bet is they will be willing to accommodate you. They are easy to reach as they are in the habit of returning phone calls. I also bet that when they hang up they will say to themselves, "Hey, great idea, maybe I should try that approach."

The company's receptionist is another excellent source of information. Receptionists are often willing to answer your questions and offer interesting tidbits. However, understand that they see a lot of one-dimensional, intrusive sales representatives come through the door, so initially they may be reluctant to help. Be professional, introduce yourself, and tell them why you need their help; you are doing your homework. You can also speak to someone who knows the workings of a company better than anybody else—it may be a foreman, a supervisor, a shipper/receiver, or a driver. These people are usually happy to chat with you.

The list of potential sources is endless. It all depends upon your creativity and commitment to the relationship. Ultimately, your potential customer will be impressed with your knowledge. It demonstrates an obvious respect for their time. Unquestionably, it's a first big step in differentiating yourself and neutralizing your competition, especially if they are hanging out at their adult daycare center being too busy to plan.

From time to time you may find yourself responding to unexpected inquiries where a potential customer has called your company. This call could be triggered by word-of-mouth, one of your advertisements, seeing you at a tradeshow, or it may be simply an inquiry. In any case, your objective is to get an appointment. Resist the temptation to *sell* them on the telephone. Sell the appointment instead. However, during the initial telephone conversation learn as much as you can about them to ascertain their potential.

If there is potential, sell the appointment and then do your homework prior to the call. A strategy that has proven very effective for me when we get unexpected inquiries is to call their receptionist and ask if he or she would mind putting together a corporate package. This may include an annual report, brochures, and other items such as a company newsletter or quarterly flyers. I then send a courier to pick up the package within 24 hours of the call. When I show up to the appointment knowledgeable about their business, customers are impressed. Once again it's about being planned and prepared.

When is the optimum time to do your planning? I'm sure you answered "during non-selling hours." Right answer. Don't use valuable selling hours to plan. As we discuss in Chapter 4, ideally your planning is done before or after selling hours, not during. However, sometimes selling hours provide the only opportunity to call receptionists or other sales entrepreneurs. Even so, use your limited selling hours wisely.

A State of Readiness

With our planning complete, we are now ready to prepare for the call. Remember, planning is stuff we do prior to the call, whereas preparation is being ready to perform at the call. A state of readiness begins by arriving on time, which means being 10 to 15 minutes early. This gives you time to mentally and physically prepare. Preparation includes not only checking your personal hygiene (fix your hair, check yourself out, look good) but your corporate hygiene as well. Corporate hygiene is not something we put much thought into. It means having the appropriate tools with you to conduct business at the call. It includes having a professional carrying case or briefcase stocked with product manuals, company literature, calculator, price list, professional notepad, and perhaps a laptop. All these corporate items contribute to the overall impression you make on your customer. Remember, the Sequential Model says that you are engineering customer commitment (closing) beginning with Step #1. Anything you do, say, display, or not display will either enhance or erode the sale. You cannot afford to sabotage your credibility through the use of cheap, unprofessional tools that contradict your objectives as a sales entrepreneur. Get rid of the 99¢ Bic pen and the $1.50 notepad that communicates, "I'm not really serious." Sweat the details. Most people can't distinguish between a $1,000 suit or a $450 one, but they can see the difference between a good pen or a cheap one. Don't let the 99¢ Bic be your signature.

What about your personal identity package? For years experts have reminded us of the tremendous impact image communicates. Your wardrobe—your business attire—speaks volumes before you speak. People buy you with their eyes within ten seconds. Appropriate apparel and impeccable grooming demonstrate respect for yourself and for your customer. They communicate authority and exemplify your commitment to perform to the high standards of a sales entrepreneur. Dress violations such as wearing white socks with a suit, a too-short tie ,or having a run in your stockings can be very distracting to your customer. Neutralize your appearance so that the focus is on you and your message. Don't draw their attention away by wearing something that speaks louder than you. You must make sure that nothing you say or display distracts from the call. You can't aim too high in the pursuit of personal and corporate hygiene. A winning combination of the two will certainly put you at an advantage and exceed the expectations of others. A footnote regarding the importance of image: Naked people have made little impression in this world. Look good, feel good, be good.

For a sales entrepreneur the highest of personal and professional standards should prevail. Planning and preparation will complement your commitment to excellence, as the standards you set will reflect the rewards you get.

A true story to illustrate the importance of readiness: A few years ago I had a sales representative call on me selling disability insurance. She had made an appointment and she arrived exactly on time. As we went through some initial pleasantries I found her likeable. Her name was Betty. About 10 to 15 minutes into the call, I asked Betty what disability insurance would cost for a fellow my age. I was interested. I recognized a need and I wanted more details. Betty's answer was, "I can't give you that information today. My computer is in the car. I will have it for you next week." I was a little annoyed. However, the conversation continued and she finally asked what I did. I love answering that question. I told her I facilitate professional selling skills seminars to sales professionals like herself. Her jaw dropped and she asked, "Oh, how am I doing?" Reluctantly, I told her she was doing terribly. "Why is your computer in the car?" I asked. What's wrong with this picture? Her defense was, "But this is my first call to you. I'm here to get to know you." That's funny, I thought she was here to sell me disability insurance. Betty seemed to think she should make a couple of social calls, then sell me. You see, Betty was guilty of minimal planning and no preparation. Clearly, she was not prepared to do business. She arrived at the call with little more than a predetermined, well-rehearsed selling strategy that did not include any precall planning. No flexibility. I have seen it applied countless times: Representatives plow their way through a sales call with little regard for the customer's agenda. I call it the "cookie-cutter" sales call. We eventually did business, but it took her more calls than necessary to close the deal. Betty and I became good friends and she still talks about her call from hell.

The Betty story is classic. I know there are countless sales representatives out there making sales calls not unlike Betty's—little planning, unprepared. I may be getting ahead of myself, but the most effort you should put into closing a sale is on the *first* call. Of course this won't happen on every occasion, especially if you have a long sales cycle (the time it takes a sale to materialize). The mindset of a sales entrepreneur is this: I'm here to sell something, not just to visit and have coffee.

Every sales call, including telephone sales calls, must be packaged around two important aspects: a primary agenda and a secondary agenda. Your primary agenda is to *sell* something—it's the number one reason you are there. Your secondary agenda is to establish rapport and build a relationship—get to know your customer. During the call, however, the sequence is reversed. First build rapport and trust (make a friend) then build on that trust by selling a solution that the customer buys. Although being friendly and building relationships are important, customers know that the reason for a sales call is a sale. Each time you speak with a customer you should have a clear objective—an action you want taken as a result of the call. You are there to do business, to advance the sale. Why do you think you were hired? Your customer expects you to pursue an opportunity to do business, otherwise you may be perceived as wasting their time. By appreciating these two aspects of a call agenda, you save yourself valuable selling time and reduce the number of wasted and unproductive sales calls. Be prepared to sell something on the first call. Don't condemn yourself to mediocrity by not planning ahead of time, like my friend Betty.

Countless sales managers, myself included, have been guilty of misguiding the activities of newly hired salespeople. They seem to forget or don't appreciate why the salesperson was hired. Their instructions to the new salesperson are, "Take the next few months to simply introduce yourself to your customers and don't be bothering them by trying to sell something. They will buy once they get to know you better." How ridiculous. What a gross violation of the company's time and money, not to mention a big injustice to the customer. Customers get irritated by calls that don't have any clear direction or provide an understanding of what comes next. Customers are often left wondering why on earth they granted an appointment. "I thought she was going to sell me something or at least show me a new product line."

Tim Commandment #3

Have clearly defined primary and secondary agenda for every sales call. Ask: What am I going to sell?

If you cannot make the sale, at least sell the *next step*. Always leave the customer's office with an agreement, a commitment for the next step. It can include a breakfast meeting, a plant tour, a call with the VP of manufacturing, a demonstration of your product, and so on. We can't afford to chew up valuable selling hours by making unnecessary return calls or return visits. Remember, studies concur that planning and preparation will reduce your sales cycle and increase productivity by a minimum of 20%. You are running a business, ME Inc. Don't work hard, sell smart.

Time to Show Off

The moment of truth. After weeks of telephone tag, voicemail, and time spent planning, you are finally face-to-face with your customer. You have precious little time to deal with the initial tension and create a positive first impression. Psychological studies concur that the best approach to build rapport and trust is to get your customers talking about themselves or their business. It's even more effective if you initiate the dialogue using information pertinent to their business. This is where you can stimulate the conversation by showing off your new-found intelligence. You have worked hard to obtain precall information about your potential customer. Don't hide it. Don't be shy or hesitant to show off. You want to be subtle yet professional. The following examples are effective openers when presented using an, "Oh, by the way" approach.

- Congratulations on the company's 10th anniversary.

- Congratulations on his or her recent promotion.

- How is your new office in Cleveland working out?

- I see you recently introduced a new product line.

- I saw your new advertisement. It looks great!

- Are you still hiring?

Tie in any knowledge you have. Be forthcoming. Your knowledge and enthusiasm communicates to the customer that he or she is important and worth the time you invested in planning.

Features and Benefits: No Advantages

The terms "feature" and "benefit" are commonly used within the sales profession but, unfortunately, they are often misused. Sales professionals frequently interchange these terms, not clear on their meaning. Feature/benefit selling represents one of the cornerstones of professional selling. It has been an effective strategy for centuries and I don't expect it to change, not in our lifetime. It's part of the common currency of every sales call.

To be an effective sales entrepreneur, you must relate your product to the prospect's unique situation. You do this by translating your features into benefits that satisfy the customer's needs. It begins with an understanding of both features and benefits.

A *feature* is defined as a quality or characteristic of your product or service: *what it has*. Simple. As part of our planning we need to recognize and appreciate the four feature categories. They are the features of:

- your industry

- your company

- your product or service

- you

Each category, of course, offers a host of features. There can be 100 features just about your company, 100 features about your industry, and so on. These features combined become your corporate menu. It's a menu of all your offerings, including you (which happens to be the most overlooked feature category). When was the last time you said to a prospect, "And another reason you should buy from us is because I'm *your* salesperson." Don't sell yourself short. Make a list of all your features. If you are uncomfortable with this exercise, go back to Chapter 2, Attitude #3.

A *benefit* is defined as what the feature does for the customer. It is how a particular feature will help a customer and is tied directly to buying motives. At the end of the day it addresses,

"Here's how I can help your business." Also, benefits must answer the proverbial question "What's in it for me?"

You may be familiar with the FAB approach of selling: features, advantages, and benefits. I have eliminated advantages. Not required. As it is, sales professionals have a tough time separating features and benefits. Let's not complicate it with an unnecessary step. Few salespeople can clearly distinguish between advantages and benefits. That being the case, how would you expect your customers to appreciate the difference? Both of you end up confused. My approach is simple. Customers buy only benefits, not advantages or features. For example, when you buy a car the feature (your hot-button) is power windows but the benefits are ease of operation, convenience, and control.

Avoid the Feature Dump

One of my favorite topics is the good old feature dump. Almost all salespeople (including sales entrepreneurs) are guilty of it. The *feature dump* is talking about what the product is, how it works, and how it compares with the competition, but *not* what it will do for the customer. Salespeople jump into a monologue, talking ad nauseam about all the features, often boring the customer to tears. Believe it or not, customers simply don't care about most of that stuff. The conversation with your potential customers often lacks the critical connection between your product, service, or company and their needs. Customers need to know how you can help improve their efficiencies or their margins, or help them become more competitive. More often than not salespeople are selling what they need to sell, instead of selling what their customers need to buy.

Typically, sales professionals show up to the call and after asking only a couple of probes begin spewing all their knowledge, telling not selling. They engage in a verbal avalanche of information, statistics, specifications, and whatever else they can think of to impress the customer. After all, salespeople are supposed to be good talkers, right? Wrong. The underlying problem is the vast amount of product knowledge that salespeople are exposed to. Companies inundate their salespeople with product knowledge, company policies, price lists, catalogs, brochures, flavor-of-the-month promotions, new product launches, and so on. It's no wonder salespeople show up and can't wait to *tell* the customer about all the features. It's what they have been trained to talk about, to regurgitate all the information in the brochure. In fact, a brochure is nothing more than a *glossy* feature dump, just as a corporate video distributed by head office is a *high-tech* feature dump. A brochure or video can't possibly reflect benefits, as they are very subjective. It is the customers' right to identify the benefits that are important to them. Customers decide the benefits, not the salespeople.

More often than not, salespeople respond far too quickly when asked for a brochure. They willingly send out or hand out their corporate brochures, creating a false sense of productivity. Tell your potential customer that *you* are better than a brochure, and a 15-minute appointment is necessary to explore the possibility of doing business.

On the lighter side, rather than spend the day handing out or mailing brochures with a business card ("Just leave us your card and a brochure") you'd be better off to rent an airplane, fly over your territory, and shovel out 1,000 brochures. It would certainly get more attention! My point is this: Doing an in-person brochure-drop does little to drive your business. Brochures should be used as a leave-behind to augment the sale—not used as a lead-in. However, they can be an effective mailer if you highlight relevant features and follow up with a telephone call to make an appointment after they have received it. This approach will sometimes impress the customer enough to grant you an appointment.

What drives the feature dump is our natural tendency to be helpful. We are often seduced by a false sense of helpfulness created by *telling* the customer all about our features. Sales representatives love to dispense information. As one customer said, salespeople tend to "show-up and throw-up." This situation reminds me of those PEZ candy dispensers we had as kids: pull the head back and all this information comes spewing out. We often get overzealous in our desire to enhance our customer's welfare. It's nothing short of blah-blah-blah selling, inundating the customer with useless information. I consider PEZ to be an acronym for "Please Excuse my Zealousness." Go out and get yourself a PEZ dispenser and put it on your desk as a visual reminder to banish the feature dump. We must appreciate that our call-effectiveness is measured in terms of the customer's perspective, not ours.

The redundancy of a feature dump is further supported by this statistic: Your customer will decide to buy from you based on *less* than 5% of your total features. That's it! If you ask your customers why they bought from you, their answer reveals no more than two to three reasons (benefits). Imagine the poor customer having to endure a feature dump that is 95% useless information to them. I compare it to the menu analogy. When you visit a restaurant, you are presented with a menu. The menu is nothing more than a list of available features. You, as the customer, decide what features will become benefits. As you are handed your menu, your server might as well say, "Here is our list of features. I'll be back in a few minutes to take your list of benefits." After reviewing the menu, which can easily include 100 or more features, you place your order of only four to five benefits. There's your 5%. The rest of the items remain as features. The only person who can decide on the benefits is your customer. Your customer is the ultimate authority to either accept or reject your features as benefits. There lies the challenge: Identify the features on your corporate menu that will benefit your customer.

Feature Dumpers Syndrome is an undetected virus that has plagued salespeople for centuries. It sabotages more sales calls than any other sales virus.

The common feature dump virus quietly goes about its business disguising itself as a routine, predictable component of a typical sales call. If you don't think you are a feature dumper, just ask your customers.

Unfortunately there are no pills, antibiotics, or prescriptions available to cure this unproductive approach to selling. But don't fret, help is here at last. The cure lies in your willingness and commitment to embrace a sales entrepreneurial code of conduct. It's time to do more selling, and less telling; features tell, benefits sell.

The feature dump is not something we can totally eliminate. From time to time you will find yourself engaged in an elaborate monologue spewing out so-what information. If you find yourself in this situation, the best thing to do is finish your thought, pause for a moment and say, "Well that's enough about me, how about telling me more about you." Invite the customer to talk about his or her business by asking conversational probes. Resist the temptation to revert back to a feature dump. Take notes and truly listen to what your customer is telling you.

Two Types of Information

One of the deadliest traps of a sales call is predictability: the mark of a boring order-taker selling on price versus value. Customers have been conditioned over the years to anticipate a boring, predictable sales call—the kind where a representative shows up and dispenses a well-rehearsed pitch. Sometimes customers themselves open the call by saying, "Okay, let's hear your pitch," or "Tell me about your company." In fact, customers often communicate their displeasure with the these routine sales calls by not granting second appointments. The first appointment must be worthwhile or you can forget about a second appointment. Some customers go as far as to say, "Okay, come in but you've only got 15 minutes." That is simply a way to shield themselves from another lengthy feature dump.

> I told him all about our company and our great products and he still didn't buy anything. Selling sucks!

What should you do if your customer looks at his watch and says that you've only got five minutes? Believe me, it happens. Sadly enough, the majority of salespeople take that as an invitation to recite the Cliff's Notes version of their pitch. If you answered, "I'd tell him all about our company and what we do," you may want to reconsider your approach. Avoid the overwhelming temptation to feature dump. During the first few seconds acknowledge the limited time frame and suggest you'll be finished in four and a half minutes. Then give the customer a 45-second infomercial as to who you are and what you do, highlighting the distinctive benefits that may be of interest. Then ask permission to ask a few questions to learn more about their business to explore if there is a possible fit. During your probing, the customer will clearly see your sincerity and obvious interest. Take the last 30 seconds to acknowledge your time is up and reschedule another appointment. I suggest that the vast majority of the time the customer will be impressed with your obvious interest and extend the appointment by saying, "It's okay, please continue." Remember, if customers feel you may be able to help their business or alleviate an existing inconvenience, they are interested. Your five-minute appointment will often turn into a one-hour conversation.

During the sales call it is the type of information being dispensed by the salesperson that labels the call as routine and boring, or interesting and worthwhile for the customer. There are two types of information. First, there is what I call so-what information, usually associated with sales representatives. It's the classic feature dump where the representative is working through a well-rehearsed, enthusiastic pitch about all the features but generating a so-what reaction from the customer. Even the sales representative gets bored with it.

The second type of information is, "Here's how I can help your business," usually associated with a sales entrepreneur. Surprisingly, this approach is a refreshing change for your customer. It breaks the typical mold of a sales call and brings something new to the table, a genuine interest in the customer. Of course this type of information just doesn't happen. It's the result of effective planning, preparation, and smart probing. Once you have identified relevant features (via probing), bridge them to the corresponding benefits. We have more on bridging and probing in Chapter 7.

I offer a statistic that should surprise you. Your competitor can offer approximately 90% of the same features you can. I call it the duplication factor. Why do you think they are called competitors? Because they duplicate many of the same things you do, maybe even better. To compete, they mirror several of the same features you offer. The key is to differentiate yourself, emphasizing that the business advantage your company can offer is *you*. Your competitors don't have you. Anyone can copy and improve a product or service, match a competitor's features, copy their sales promotions, or undercut prices, but they can't copy or duplicate *you*. Apply your own unique style, your own signature, to your Sequential Model. Remember, customers are looking to buy relationships (peace of mind), not just products.

I don't mean to suggest that product knowledge is not important. Of course it is. I agree that you must know what you are talking about in terms of specifications, technical applications, manufacturing specifications, industry standards, and your competitors' offerings. Learn as much about your competitors as you can. Make it part of your planning. However, although this information is important, it won't close a sale for you. Remember, only 20% of the decision to buy from you is based on your product knowledge.

Account Classification: Three Types

Managing your account base is often a question of maintaining existing customers and finding new customers who are most likely to buy, then engaging your resources to maximize the opportunity. However, some accounts are more profitable than others and let's face it, profit drives your business. You must maximize your returns by satisfying the greatest number of profitable customers. Return can be measured in a number of ways: ROI (return on investment)—the amount of money and time spent on an account; ROE (return on energy)—energy expended to secure the account; ROO (return on occasion)— leads or referrals you get while golfing or participating at an occasion outside normal selling activities or selling hours. ROO extends your limited selling hours and ROT (return on your time equity)—asks how wisely are you spending your allotted time.

Not all customers have the same buying potential. The portion of unprofitable accounts is usually greater than you think. I remind you of the 80/20 rule: 80% of your sales come from only 20% of your customers. Therefore, sales entrepreneurs need to classify customers on the basis of their sales potential, to avoid spending too much time with low-potential accounts. Remember, there are only 1,760 selling hours in one entire year. We can't afford to be busy servicing unproductive, unprofitable accounts. Don't be fooled by revenue numbers. Revenue alone doesn't keep a business afloat, profits do. Pricing your product or service at or below cost is not smart business, but many sales representatives are seduced into a quick sale where profit is sacrificed for revenue. Your business must be managed by utilizing all of the resources at your disposal, maximizing your return in the most productive manner. To that end I offer a very simple account classification strategy: the ABC analysis. It's not new but it certainly works. Use this method to evaluate and classify each of your existing and potential accounts.

A Accounts

Your A accounts deserve the most attention. Here's why:

- They have high potential return: (ROI/ROE/ROO/ROT)

- They require minimum invested time

- They are low maintenance
- They are cooperative if problems arise
- They have a high contribution based on margins/profit
- They have a short sales cycle

B Accounts

B accounts are not quite as attractive as your As, but certainly worth pursuing. Here's why:

- They have good potential return: (ROI/ROE/ROO/ROT)
- They require a high amount of invested time
- They have higher maintenance
- They are patient with problems
- They have a good contribution based on margins/profit
- They have a longer sales cycle

C Accounts

I fondly refer to a C account as "a pain in the asset." C accounts usually distract you from your A and B accounts, offering little or no return for your investment. Here's why:

- They offer low/no potential return: (ROI/ROE/ROO/ROT)
- They require an excessive amount of time
- They are high maintenance, lots of babysitting
- They are impatient when problems arise
- They provide minimal contribution based on low or no margins/profits
- They have very long sales cycle

These accounts are literally a pain. They whine about this and that, finding the darndest things to complain about. In spite of your efforts they are never satisfied.

As you classify your accounts, I strongly recommend you continue to work closely with your As and Bs, and toss your Cs. That's right, get rid of them. With limited selling hours, you can't possibly maintain C accounts as well as service your As and Bs. Remember, C accounts are a major distraction to your core business accounts. By responding to or pursuing C accounts, your A/B accounts could inadvertently become a silver platter opportunity for your competitor. In most cases the neglect is unintentional but the consequences can be dire. This is a chief cause of lost customers.

However, be aware of potential changes in account status. A C account today may become an A account tomorrow. Likewise a B today may become a C tomorrow, and so on. There is no universal grading system. An A or B account in your territory could well be a C in another territory. Each territory has its own unique account classification parameters.

Here is a fact that may help guide your thinking as you manage and grow your account base. It costs your employer approximately $200 to $300 for every sales call you make (based on approximately one hour of actual selling time). Now let's add $200 for the customer's time and we have a $500 sales call. Not many salespeople think in terms of cost per sales call but as an entrepreneur, you must ask yourself, "Is this call worth $500?" It becomes clear that time with a C account is not only unproductive, but very costly.

Once you have determined that an account has a C status, don't be too quick to abandon it. Four options are available.

1. **Use them to practice.** Where do most salespeople practice and refine their sales skills? Usually when they are sitting

before an A or B customer. Not a good plan. Practice the steps of your Sequential Model at a C account. It's a win-win situation. If you screw up, the customer won't want to do business with you anyway. The big win is that you took a step closer to refining and polishing your skills in a low-risk situation. Practice makes permanent—no different than a professional golfer hitting hundreds of balls at the driving range. A C account is to a sales entrepreneur what a flight simulator is to a pilot developing a new skill.

2. **Double their price.** I don't necessarily mean literally double it, but certainly a price increase may be appropriate. Visit or call your C accounts with their revised pricing in your hot little hand. No doubt their reaction will be, "Look at this, you increased my price." Your response is, "Yes, I know." The revised price represents the lowest point at which you will do business with them. It's your line in the sand. Anything lower and you are simply not interested. The upside can be rewarding. If they accept your revised price, you now have a B or an A account. It is surprising how often they accept the revised pricing—and if they do be sure to nurture them to a solid B or possibly an A account.

    Another response you may hear from a C account is, "I can buy it cheaper elsewhere." That could very well be true and the natural tendency of a sales representative is to reduce the price until the customer agrees to buy. However, if the customer is unhappy with your lowest price-point, I suggest you use Lee Iaccoca's line: "If you feel you can get a better deal elsewhere, then buy it." It communicates confidence in yourself and your proposal and quite often customers will reevaluate their decision. Customers today appreciate the old adage, "You get what you pay for."

3. **Clean deal.** Logic tells us that with limited selling hours we simply can't extend your C customers the luxury of a personal sales call. Explain to them that their situation does not justify or warrant a personal visit. You will no longer make the one-hour trek to visit them. It's simply not a good validation of your 1,760 selling hours. Inform your customer that you are prepared to sell to them, but without direct representation. However, the condition of doing business is that you redefine the rules of engagement. These would include pricing, a delivery schedule, minimum order quantities, and payment terms.

    Once both parties understand the new arrangement, invite them to place orders with your order desk or inside representative. Or they may want to send you an e-mail order or leave a voice mail. This approach can be effective and represents a clean deal for both you and your customers. Also, it can be an additional revenue stream that contributes to your monthly, quarterly, or annual targets.

4. **Fire them.** During my years of selling I have never seen a concept so openly embraced by the business community. Fire C accounts. Companies are no longer tolerant of the aggravations and frustrations C accounts bring. Case in point: I recently called on one of my national accounts and asked how his morning was going. He said this, "I spent the morning deciding which accounts to fire." This comment echoes the sentiments of corporate executives. Sales managers have typically challenged salespeople to close every possible account within their territory. They constantly ask, "Are we doing business there and if not, why not?" Managers should now be asking, "*Why* are we doing business there?" I encourage sales managers to challenge their

salespeople—ask them to validate, with sound justification, why an account is doing business with them. Just because an account resides in your territory doesn't mean you have to come hither to their beckoning call. You can pick and choose who qualifies to do business with you. Establish the parameters for your A and B accounts and know what parameters flag a C account. I recently made a sales call and the manager I was visiting had an interesting analogy. The company was in the process of "demarketing" its account base. It was eliminating the Cs and focusing on its As and Bs.

Firing an account doesn't mean pursuing an unprofessional, unceremonious approach. It means engaging in an open, honest dialogue with your customer. It could be as simple as saying, "Although we have both explored the possibility of doing business together, it appears at this time we cannot move forward. I do thank you for considering us." You then suggest the customer research the market for other options. Appreciating how valuable your time is, your choice is simple. You can choose to work more and make less, or work less and make more.

Another aspect to consider is to evaluate each opportunity within existing accounts. Evaluate and classify each opportunity based on its own merit. Don't throw out the baby with the bath water. For example, you may be presented with a C opportunity within an A account. Your options are to fulfil the C opportunity in the interest of the relationship, or to politely decline by explaining your reasons and perhaps suggesting an alternative. An effective strategy is when you and your customer *agree to disagree.* Rather than aggravating your customer by walking away from a C opportunity, it's preferable to openly discuss your reasons. Come to an agreement and that may be to disagree, all the while keeping the relationship intact.

Parameters that flag a C account or C opportunities are as varied as customers themselves. Typical reasons include poor returns, they insist on a rock-bottom price, they are too demanding, you are unable to fulfil expectations, or they order lower-than-acceptable volumes. However, you may elect to pursue them for corporate or political reasons as the Head Office may deem the account prestigious or strategic to the business—one that looks great on the corporate résumé.

*Congratulations, you have now completed
Step #2*

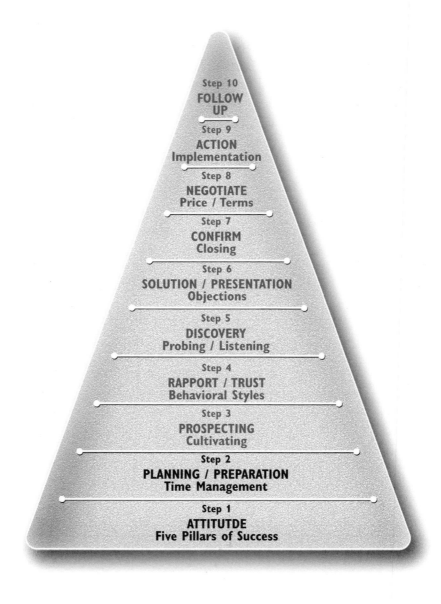

Step 10
FOLLOW
UP

Step 9
ACTION
Implementation

Step 8
NEGOTIATE
Price / Terms

Step 7
CONFIRM
Closing

Step 6
SOLUTION / PRESENTATION
Objections

Step 5
DISCOVERY
Probing / Listening

Step 4
RAPPORT / TRUST
Behavioral Styles

Step 3
PROSPECTING
Cultivating

Step 2
PLANNING / PREPARATION
Time Management

Step 1
ATTITUTDE
Five Pillars of Success

Chapter 4

TIME MANAGEMENT: IT'S ABOUT TIME

A mentor of mine once told me, "People make time for things they want to do." If someone doesn't want to participate, it ain't gonna happen. Back to the dynamics of motivation: Only you can light a fire within (Chapter 2). We must take responsibility for ourselves and our actions, and use SMART goals to stimulate motivation. Motivation is the difference between being proactive and in control, or being reactive, out of control. Become the author of your activities and your success. Make things happen rather than just reacting to events as they occur. The choice is simple: Either manage time and invest it wisely, or time will control you.

But I Don't Have Time!

How often have you wished for only "a few more hours" in your day? How many times have you searched for a magic answer, a quick fix, to relieve the pressures of time? If you are like most of us, the answer is: frequently. We live in an environment of unfinished tasks, half-done sales plans, incomplete reports, unread books, and endless personal chores. There is no question that the majority of us are time-starved, always running "just a bit behind." Would a 30-hour day help? I doubt it. It would just add six more hours of accumulated stress and frustration to our lives. Let's do a better job of managing the time we have.

In Chapter 2, you learned about five attitudinal characteristics of sales entrepreneurs and the impact those characteristics have on performance, personally and professionally. This attitudinal package—including time management—forms the backbone of the skills discussed throughout the model. Within the Sequential Model, however, time management is not a step on its own, although I do feel the subject is worthy of a chapter.

On the wishlist of salespeople's training topics, time management continues to dominate, as if there exists a magic answer, a quick fix to exonerate them from the necessary discipline required to be organized: the discomfort of discipline. Once again we tend to search for the easy way, the path of least resistance. The quick fix is available but not in pill form, not yet. It comes in the form of commitment and desire, coupled with the attitudinal package discussed in Step #1 of the sequential model.

The first step on the road to recovery is to recognize that *you* are the one primarily responsible for your own time problems and frustrations. Don't continue to rely on a plethora of well-rehearsed excuses to bail you out. The next step is to truly have the desire and the commitment to invest whatever is necessary to become organized. Without these ingredients, time management will continue to be a laborious exercise in futility and frustration, robbing you of your full potential.

By the way, you *do* have enough time.

Time Equity: What's Your ROT?

Time is a unique, unrenewable resource. It marches onward at a rate of 60 minutes every hour. It shows no favoritism. No one is immune to the relentless, unforgiving passage of time.

Consider this: two days from now, tomorrow will be yesterday. Or how about this: two days ago, yesterday was tomorrow. Confused? Read it again, you'll see. Warning: dates on the calendar are closer than they appear.

In today's competitive environment, workloads have become swollen by increasingly leaner and meaner companies. There are fewer positions on company organizational charts, and the average workload of those who remain has been growing. Salespeople now have to spend more time in the office distracted from selling by fulfilling administrative obligations. You must appreciate that companies today pay for results, not the number of hours you work. Companies no longer reward busyness. In many cases, working long hours, a 60- or 70-hour week, is simply a smoke screen concealing inefficiencies and poor work habits. Nothing is easier than being busy, and few things are more difficult than being efficient and effective. It requires discipline. Imagine having the time to get your work done, leaving the office at a reasonable hour, and spending the rest of your day with family or friends. It's possible; read on.

The one universal distribution of equity is *time:* Everybody on the planet has ownership of 24 hours per day. We all receive the same allotment, day in and day out. Each new day brings an automatic deposit of 24 hours into our "time account." I refer to it as *time equity.* Although each day brings a new deposit, each day the entire amount must be withdrawn, with no balance carried over to tomorrow. Use it or lose it. The challenge we face is how and where to invest our time equity. These decisions determine success, career path, productivity, and family status. The truth is that where we are in life is a direct reflection of how well we have managed our time portfolio—how and where we "spent our time." We often hear people refer to personal activities in terms of time equity: "How did you spend your weekend?" or "During our trip we spent a lot of time doing . . ." Time equity is the essence of a full and complete life. We often take it for granted and succumb to its harsh, unforgiving consequences. We have to take responsibility for ourselves and consciously appreciate the positive impact time management can have on our lives.

Anyone who expects to achieve sales success should expect to make a serious commitment to working hard and efficiently. Throughout the five principles of time management that follow I share various techniques and suggestions to help streamline your activities. Remember we discussed *balance* in Chapter 2. Think of your activities in terms of quality and quantity. Balance means quality time versus quantity time. Many people spend *quantity* time in the office, but not *quality* time.

What's your return on time (ROT)? You own it; invest it wisely.

Five Principles of Time Management

Time cannot think for you, but it can certainly work for you. Like any other investment, time produces returns if invested wisely and treated with respect. Sales professionals constantly explore investment opportunities for their time, maximizing their ROT.

Principle #1: Maximize Your ROT

Spending your time wisely starts with paying attention to *how* you spend it. Only when you decide to take control of your time will you have the power to stop squandering it. The best starting point to a better ROT is to conduct your own time-efficiency study. Evaluate your current use of time by breaking down a typical day into hourly increments. Be objective. Include everything throughout your entire day, even the time you sleep. You may need to track a full week or two to get a clear picture of your time usage. The tape recorder you purchased after reading Chapter 2 might be a convenient method to log your time. It won't take long for patterns or habits to emerge. Some will be painfully obvious and you'll need no encouragement to change. We improve our ROT only by recognizing how we *spend* our time.

The next step is to review your time log and classify the activities as time-wasters, obligations, or priorities. *Time-wasters* are just that, activities that distract you and contribute nothing toward your goals. Eliminate them. The danger is that time-wasters are activities performed out of habit. Usually, they create a false sense of productivity but actually produce few or no results. The cure comes in the form of personal organization, the process of incorporating structure into your day.

Obligations are the dutiful responsibilities of your job. They are necessary yet unimportant activities, usually performed throughout the day. They contribute indirectly to your goals. They are the administrative aspects of your job such as call reports, expense reports, quarterly forecasts, and various other required duties. Despite the challenges of limited time coupled with increased responsibilities, you can be productive by evaluating your current usage of your 24 hours and maximizing ROT. Obligations cannot be overlooked but be cognizant of the negative impact they have on daily productivity. As you become better organized you can streamline your activities, minimizing the time spent fulfilling obligations. You may be in a position to delegate some of your administrative duties to support people (internal customers) within your office. I know of some sales entrepreneurs who have hired a part-time assistant. Maximize your ROT by doing what you do best, selling.

Priorities are the activities that contribute significantly to your ROT. They are directly responsible for your results, moving you closer to your goals. Remember, companies today pay for results, not activities. They no longer pay for attendence, they expect results.

As you evaluate your current use of time, the time-wasters will become clear, allowing you to rethink your activities. Make the shift from a long day filled with unproductive busyness to a shorter day focusing on priorities. As a sales entrepreneur, challenge yourself to be more proactive by prioritizing your tasks. Take control of the activities that prey on your efficiency, compromising your ROT. Once you complete your time-efficiency study, you will be shocked to see the time wasted reacting to other people's demands and requests. Most of us habitually spend our days *reacting* instead of being proactive, unaware of the costly consequence. I suggest that up to 75% of our day is reactive. A sobering thought.

Principle #2: Know What Time It Is

If you are like most salespeople, you have too much to do and not enough time to get it all done. To get ahead in today's fast-paced world, you've got to be aware of what time it is. I'm not talking about telling time, you learned that years ago. What I'm talking about is: It's not enough that you're doing a particular job right, you've got to be sure that you're doing the right activity at the right time. By the way, if you don't have a good watch, get one. The best and simplest time management tool is on your wrist. Common sense tells us that we should spend the majority of our time working on high-priority A and B accounts.

Most of us don't. We waste a lot of time in the adult daycare center reacting to the demands of C accounts or even performing C activities. The first step is to take control of your entire day by knowing what time it is.

Selling Hours or Janitorial Hours?

A full year gives us time equity of 8,760 hours. The use of these hours is a personal choice under our direct control. However, one thing we cannot control is the number of available *selling* hours in a year. There are approximately 1,760 *selling* hours in one entire year. That's all. A rather sobering statistic. Here's the math: Your customers work approximately eight hours a day and there are approximately 220 selling days per year (8 x 220 = 1,760). The 220 selling days is the number of business days minus weekends, holidays, and wasted time throughout the year, including travel time and doing personal chores during the business day. These numbers may vary depending upon industry, but for the sake of discussion I use 1,760.

During valuable selling hours you must organize yourself to maximize face-time or talk-time. Don't perform administrative obligations during selling time. Do those activities during the *janitorial hours,* outside the 8 AM to 5 PM selling hours. Having worked with large and small companies, I've often witnessed salespeople who don't appreciate what time it is. I see them in the adult daycare center during the day doing their expense reports or call reports, updating customer files, and performing general administrative obligations. There are approximately 4,400 janitorial hours in a year: the time available to perform your administrative tasks. Successful sales entrepreneurs know that selling is not an 8 AM to 5 PM job. They carefully plan their days to maximize selling time, and use the after-hours time to complete administrative activities. So, next time you're thinking of getting your hair cut, getting the car washed, or doing your expense report during selling hours, refer to Tim Commandment #3, Page 71.

Principle #3: Manage Your Time

Time management is a personal process. It takes a strong commitment to change long-established habits. According to the 80/20 rule, we get 80% of our results from 20% of the things we do. This statistic supports the observation that we spend a lot of time on time-wasters and obligations. Imagine the impact on our time efficiency if we increased the 20% to 30%!

What takes us from a time-starved day of routine, frustration, and stress to a productive day filled with accomplishments? Change. One definition of time management is doing fewer things in less time. Wouldn't that be great?

Research suggests that effective time management strategies can free up a minimum of two hours per day. For example, time management studies show that we spend up to 70 minutes a day just looking for stuff.[1] How many times have you said, "Just a minute, I know it's here somewhere." We misplace files, reports, memos, and letters, and our desks look like the movie *Twister* was filmed in our office. Clutter can be a huge time-waster, not to mention the embarrassment of lost or unanswered requests. Your goal isn't to have a nice neat desk, but to get organized so that you can convert wasted time into productive time. However, with a clean, orderly desk, you'll improve your time working on priorities that will make you money. Your quality of work will also improve.

The underlying objective of effective time management is to utilize all available resources to increase face-time, the time spent talking face-to-face with existing customers or potential cus-tomers. If you're an inside salesperson, increase talk-time. Take some time to determine how much time you actually spend with customers. Take a stop watch and clock total face-time in one entire week. On average, it's only two to four hours.[2] Shocking! This statistic serves as additional proof of the inordi-nate amount of time consumed by time-wasters and obligations. I recognize that with leaner companies salespeople are often sad-dled with more of the administrative aspects of the job. Unfortunately they become high-priced administrators. This brings us to Tim Commandment #4.

Tim Commandment #4
Manage your time equity.
Ask: Is this activity the best use
of my time right now?

How many times a day should you ask yourself if you are making the best use of your time? If you answered "several," you're right. Only you can answer that question honestly. As the president of ME Inc., don't compromise your ROT by blindly filling your day with busyness. Restructure your day to eliminate the time-wasters and minimize the time spent fulfilling obliga-tions. Sometimes working in the office on a project or on a pre-sentation could very well be the best use of your time. I doubt that you can ever eliminate time spent in the adult daycare center, but you certainly need to minimize it. Use janitorial time to fulfil your obligations.

As part of your time-efficiency study, you should determine the time of day that you are most efficient and productive. Know your *peak time,* the time of day you are at high energy. Not everyone has the same peak time. Some of us are morning people and others are afternoon or evening people. Pay attention to your moods and high-energy time of day to determine when you're most productive. Morning people can accomplish more simply by getting up an hour earlier each day, and night owls can carve out time for administrative activities in the evenings.

Once you have identified your peak time, do your worst jobs then. They won't go away so you might as well get them done when you're feeling energized. Some authors suggest doing them first thing in the morning when you're feeling fresh. This approach works well if you're a morning person but could be disastrous if you're an afternoon person. Imagine doing your worst job at your worst time of day. Two "worsts" don't make a right! In my case, prime time is during the late afternoon and early evening. I prefer to schedule important meetings or presentations later in the day, anytime after 2 PM. I did most of my writing for this book between 3 PM and 9 PM.

Another suggestion in the interest of maximizing your ROT is to learn how to say *no*. Many of us are our own worst enemies. You'll never have enough time to finish your own tasks if you're always taking on more than time permits. Don't be afraid to politely refuse a request or task if your plate is already full. This includes saying no to your sales manager. When given a task, simply ask your manager, "Would you like me to do this now or would you prefer I spend the time selling?" Your manager may decide to delegate the task elsewhere. It's great to want to help others, but not at the expense of ME Inc.

Principle #4: Use the Right Tools

A professional (sales entrepreneurs included) is anyone paid to perform a task or a job at an acceptable level of proficiency while utilizing the tools of the trade to enhance efficiency and effectiveness. I am amazed at how often I see salespeople conducting business with inappropriate tools. It's as though they're exempt from the requirement to be a professional. Imagine your doctor or dentist using anything but the best instruments. Your customers expect no less of you. As a sales entrepreneur, you have an obligation to invest in the best. You may have heard it before, "A carpenter is only as good as his tools."

The solution begins with a personal planner—a time management system that offers the convenience of portability while organizing your activities, mapping your week and, most importantly, planning your day. A good planner includes twelve months at-a-glance, 365 individual day-pages, a daily to-do list section, and an appointments section. Some planners come with a rigid set of instructions, so pick a planner that offers simplicity and the flexibility to meet your personal preferences.

A planner used effectively not only buys you time, it helps you stay in balance throughout your week, including weekends. Poor time management skills result in overspending your time, running out of day before you get everything done. I compare it to managing a checking account. Imagine opening a checking account at your local bank then not using a checkbook to track the account activity. Surely you would find yourself out of balance at the end of the month, possibly overspending your available funds. Without the appropriate tool to track your time-related activities, you quickly find yourself out of balance, overdrawn on your time account.

Sales Automation

What's the best time management tool for the sales entrepreneur: the almighty computer or the personal planner? The debate continues. I have witnessed and have been a part of many lively discussions weighing legitimate pros and cons of the laptop computer as a time management tool.

My position is this: Computers are great for certain tasks but time management isn't one of them. In spite of all our wonderful technologies it appears that the good old pencil and paper system is still viable. More and more professionals who were initially romanced by time management software programs are returning to the convenience, simplicity, and portability of the personal planner. I'm not suggesting people are littering our highways with abandoned laptops, but they are learning to work in harmony with a laptop or a palm pilot *and* pencil and paper. The ideal system seems to be a combination. It's no longer an either-or decision. Don't compromise your productivity by restricting yourself to only one system. Incorporate the tools that work best for you, maximizing your limited selling hours. Caution: Donít get overly seduced by technology and look like some sort of technological rambo. KISS.

Bear in mind that my comments are directed at outside salespeople. I appreciate that a computer-based time management program may be appropriate for inside salespeople, while a portable time-management system may be redundant. However, you may want to consider a smaller version of a personal planner or a palm pilot to organize your activities outside the office.

As a sales entrepreneur, your computer should be viewed as a portable database, allowing you to work in the field and access or update customer files utilizing a good contact management program. This allows you to retrieve important information prior to your appointment, including current account data, inventory levels at the warehouse, available shipping dates, price levels, and data specific to your customer. You can also store and retrieve such pieces of information as the name of your customer's spouse and children, dates of their birthdays and anniversaries, hobbies, outside interests, and favorite summer activities. You decide what data are relevant. There are several good contact management programs available. I prefer Maximizer and ACT, because both programs offer a host of features to manage your account base, saving valuable selling time.

The computer can be a great asset when utilized outside the customer's office, but it can become a liability in the customer's office. Sometimes a laptop just isn't convenient and may even be cumbersome, intrusive, and time-consuming. Laptops should be used in a customer's office only with permission, whereas you don't need permission to work with a planner. The big plus of a planner is that it's quick, convenient, portable, and useable anytime, anywhere.

Principle #5: Be Proactive, not Reactive

I would suggest that up to 75% of our day is spent reacting to the needs and requests of other people such as customers, managers, internal customers, family, and friends. We are constantly bombarded with demands on our limited time, leaving us unable to accomplish our own goals and objectives. No wonder we feel the frustration of, "So much to do, so little time."

We often succumb to the demands and requests of others because we think it is socially inappropriate to say no. We become victimized by others who may have a strong interest in controlling our activities or behavior—such as a spouse or a manager. Unfortunately many people, including salespeople, are content to be regulated and manipulated rather than committing to SMART goals and living life guided by *their* agenda, not someone else's. No one ever accomplished a personal goal by being subservient to others. Successful sales entrepreneurs refuse to be swayed by the whims of others and are quietly effective at managing their own agendas. Employers and managers some-times do more to demotivate rather than to motivate. Demotivation can take the form of intimidation or high-performance expecta-tions constrained by rigid management policies and limited resources to perform the job. No wonder so many people want to take this job and shove it.

A proactive strategy means developing the discipline to stay focused on your agenda, your goals, and your objectives. Part of this discipline comes in the form of qualifying the severity of a problem prior to reacting to it. For example, next time a cus-tomer informs you of a problem or a concern, resist the temp-tation to immediately jump into react mode, drop what you are doing, and race over to console your customer. It may not be necessary. The next time you get an irate customer (or internal customer) demanding to see you right away, follow these two steps:

1. **Acknowledge the problem.** Allow the customer to vent by explaining the situation and then clarify your understanding of it by paraphrasing. Be sure to take notes of your discus-sion for future reference. By acknowledging the concern and showing empathy, the customer will begin to feel better about it and may become somewhat flexible as to how and when you resolve the concern. A sympathetic attitude to a real or imaginary product or service failure cannot be overemphasized. A 10-minute phone call to determine the facts and the seriousness of the problem may be a valuable investment, possibly saving you hours of unnecessary run-ning around. Work smart, not hard.

2. **Suggest another time.** Tell the customer that your day is full with appointments and commitments and ask if first thing tomorrow morning would be okay to get together. Your business and time are just as important and legitimate

as that of your customer. You are equals. In the majority of cases, your customer will appreciate your schedule and agree to meet with you the next day. Too often we assume that we must respond immediately, but by following these steps you will save yourself valuable time. Sometimes, however, the customer may be insistent that you respond immediately, in which case you must act accordingly.

Another good tactic is to start building flexibility into your day. By this I mean schedule your day to allow for "poop happens." Allow time between appointments or activities to deal with interruptions that are sure to occur. Interruptions and problems are a natural component of everybody's day so don't ignore the fact that they happen, and plan accordingly. Don't try to pack too much into one day by scheduling consecutive appointments and meetings. Plan what you can reasonably expect to get accomplished that day and allow time to deal with inevitable interruptions. I suggest that you let the 60/40 rule be your guide; don't plan more than 60% of your day. The remaining 40% is reserved to deal with unforeseen yet inevitable interruptions. It also helps prevent the list-layover syndrome where we put unfinished to-do items onto tomorrow's schedule. If your workday is ten hours, don't plan for more than six hours. Once again, if you pack too much into a day, you will surely have to make rigorous cuts, deal with unfinished tasks, and wrestle with unnecessary stress. Remember, one of the aspects of a SMART goal is "attainable." Make your daily activities attainable.

If You're on Time, You're Late

This concept needs to be taken literally. Punctuality is certainly one of several prerequisites to a successful meeting, but it doesn't seem to be taken very seriously. Many salespeople arrive at appointments with barely 30 seconds to spare before sitting before a potential A or B opportunity. Not a wise thing to do. We are all time-starved, but don't compensate for it at the expense of short-changing mental preparation time. If you have a 10:00 AM meeting, be there no later than 9:50. Don't come flying in at 9:59, out of breath, and still dealing with road rage. You need those few minutes to *mentally* prepare for the meeting. Although you are there physically, you are not there mentally. You may even want to take a few minutes in the washroom to give yourself a final check before the meeting.

Don't be late. Customers accept very few excuses for tardiness—bad weather doesn't cut it. I once overheard a sales manager quip to a rep who was 15 minutes late for a meeting: "There are only two 8 o'clocks in the day. How can you screw it up?" If you are unavoidably late, even by one minute, call ahead to inform the customer of the situation. It's very professional and it's appreciated.

Embrace Stress: A Timely Suggestion

One of the biggest, most transparent time-wasters is stress. When we experience stress, it can handicap our performance and distract us. We typically experience a low energy level. Stress intrudes on our time efficiency and reduces our level of productivity. To some extent stress is inevitable and beyond our control, but how we handle it is well within our control. A five-year study published by the Families and Work Institute showed that growing demands at work are creating problems at home for time-starved employees. They end up feeling too stressed to work efficiently. Growing pressures on employees often negatively affect home lives and in turn, work lives. The study goes on to say that a high percentage of employees *always* feel they don't have enough time for their families or other important people in their lives because of their jobs, and 61% sometimes feel that way[3]. A recent survey by KPMG found that 57% of the 1,216 respondents were ambivalent about their current jobs, whereas only 25% were very satisfied. No question that this level of indifference creates stress and an attitude of frustration. For many, stress is a cause of deteriorating health, decreased productivity, and poor time management. The way I see it is some people show up to work dealing with *sleep rage* and/or *road rage,* and then go home frustrated by *job rage*—and then more *road rage.* What a day! Consider this; what tires most in life is not what we are doing, but the thought of what we haven't done yet.

So, what is stress? Stress is our *response* to various events or situations: stress is a *reaction.* The cause, or stressor, is neutral. Stress is often viewed as the enemy, a debilitating virus that cripples our productivity and unknowingly robs us of our precious time-equity. Stress has negative connotations. Libraries and bookstores are full of stress management strategies. However, stress can be positive, too. Stress may be the high level of anxiety we feel during a change in our lives, or it may be the keen sense of concentration we experience when faced with an exciting new challenge out of our comfort zone.

Stress is a great motivator. We can be motivated toward something (positive stress) or motivated away from something (negative stress). Positive stress keeps us focused, motivated, energized, and challenged. It can have tremendous impact on the efficient use of our allotted time-equity. Positive stress can enhance our performance at work and at home. When faced with a stressor, we need to remember that we can control our response. We have the "response-ability" to transform the reaction into a response that is positive. We also have the response-ability to lower our stress tolerance. In his book, *Don't Sweat the Small Stuff . . . and It's All Small Stuff,* Dr. Richard Carlson says that, "Our stress level will be exactly that of our tolerance to stress." In other words, people who say, "I can handle lots of stress" will always be under a great deal of it. It's no surprise then that people continue to take on new things until they max out their stress level. Carlson suggests the solution is to reduce our tolerance to stress. He goes on to say, "When you're feeling out of control and resentful of all you have to do, a good strategy is to relax, take a few deep breaths, and take a break." He suggests reorganizing your day and not worrying that you won't get it all done. "When your mind is clear and peaceful and your stress level is reduced, you'll be more effective and you'll have more fun."[4] I agree. I suggest you lower your stress tolerance by exercising one of the 3 Ds: do it, delegate it, or dump it. Learn how to say no. Stop taking on more than you are physically or mentally able to handle. If you find yourself overwhelmed (and who hasn't?), break down your projects into smaller, manageable parts, then assign yourself SMART goals with deadlines. Most tasks can be broken down into smaller parts, thus eliminating the need to commit to a huge uninterrupted chunk of time. As you may have heard: "How do you eat an elephant? One bite at a time." So make your time management motto this: Inch by inch, anything's a cinch.

Another way to help you put more control and less stress back into your life is to follow these four sequential steps:

1. **Identify the source.** What is causing the stress, what are the stressors? Examine your environments, both work and play, and isolate potential stressors. Explore all areas of your life.

2. **Recognize the symptoms.** What symptoms are you experiencing because of the stress: losing weight, gaining weight, drinking or smoking more, general poor health? Everybody reacts differently to stress. Know your body and how it reacts.

3. **Create solutions.** What can you change, what can you do differently? You are in full control of initiating change. Other than death, taxes, and who your parents and siblings are, you can change almost anything. You have full control over your destiny—no one else does. If you don't like your job, change it. Don't like the city you live in? Change it. Don't like your level of education? Change it.

4. **Set SMART goals.** What is your action plan for change? Set a course of action that will eventually bring about change. It won't happen overnight. Distractions can be a major deterrent to getting things done. Identify what is distracting, and find ways to eliminate it. No question that stress continues to be a virus that robs us of valuable face-time with potential customers. My overall suggestion is to identify your stressor and get rid of it. Sure, easier said than done—but get off your butt and JUST DID IT!

Let's Do Lunch: Meal Protocol

Next time you say, "Let's do lunch," you may want to consider how it relates to your ROT. Effective time management is a discipline that must be practiced every day, all day—including meals. The three meals of the day offer an excellent opportunity to extend your selling hours and possibly increase your productivity.

With an eye to that end, I offer you these guidelines on meal protocol and maximizing your meal time with customers:

Breakfast. A great way to begin the day with a potential or existing customer. Meet at 6:30 or 7:00 AM at a spot conveniently located close to their office. The dialogue should be 90% business, 10% social. You are there to sell the customer and through open conversation, discover how to earn their business. Your agenda is, "I want your business, how do I go about earning it?" Don't be afraid to express your intentions. The conversation will quickly move to business and they expect you to be asking questions. Breakfast is quick, it's cheap, and it provides excellent one-on-one time with your customer. It offers a more relaxed venue than the office and may inspire the customer to share some valuable information. Give it a try—it works well.

Lunch. What should be on our agenda when we "do lunch"? The primary objective of lunch is to thank them for their business. Don't do lunch until *after* you are doing business with them. During lunch the dialogue should be 40% business ("Thank you for your business. I want to continue our relationship by exploring other opportunities") and 60% social. Humanize the relationship and learn about some of their hobbies and interests. Personally, I will not do lunch with a customer until we have had an opportunity to do business together. Lunch can easily be seen as an attempt to buy their business.

Dinner. A great way to truly get to know your customer and show your appreciation. The dialogue should be 10% business and 90% social. The 10% business is simply to acknowledge their importance as customers and say thank you—leave it at that and enjoy the evening. However, if the customer wants to talk shop all night, go with it—it's their evening. You might want to consider planning some social topics to safeguard against any extended periods of silence. Also, I suggest you make dinner a foursome—include spouses or significant others.

"Where did the time go?" is a cry frequently heard among sales professionals working under the stress of increased demands. The answer lies in the daily application of five time-management principles to organize your life, using your time in the best possible way. Through effective allocation and organization of your time, you will have more control over your activities and reap the benefits of a proactive approach. The sooner *you* make the decision to take action, the sooner you'll have more time to enjoy life and experience less stress. At the end of the day it comes down to three options: do it, delegate it, or dump it. Enjoy your new-found freedom and the rewards of effective time management. Work to live—don't live to work

NOTES

1. Taylor, Harold. Time Management Seminar. Calgary, Alberta. 1993.

2. Author Research.

3. The Calgary Herald. *Employee Stress* Cuts Productivity, Study Declares. April 15, 1998.

4. Carlson, Richard. Ph.D. *Don't Sweat the Small Stuff . . . and it's all small stuff.* Page 53-54, 1997. Hyperion.

Chapter 5

PROSPECTING: I KNOW
WHERE YOU ARE HIDING

Remember playing the game hide-and-seek as a child? It was quite gratifying to find the person within the allotted time and then outsmart your friends by hiding where they would never find you. Well, in professional selling, you and your competitor are constantly engaged in a different kind of hide-and-seek. It's called prospecting—corporate hide-and-seek. Potential customers are out there, located in various geographical pockets throughout your territory. Success goes to the one who is most creative in finding and developing new customers, new markets.

Many sales experts and authors suggest that prospecting is the most important activity within the Sequential Model. Filling your sales funnel is the key to your economic survival. Your *sales funnel* is your inventory of potential customers. Through prospecting, customers enter your funnel as qualified, potential A or B accounts, each with its own sales cycle. Every customer has different viscosity, the time it takes to flow through the funnel and become an active account.

The emphasis on prospecting can vary among various selling fields but at the end of the day your success is determined by the quantity and quality of customers in your funnel. Constant prospecting and cultivation of your market, be it local or global, is the lifeblood of any business. All other activities center around your ability to keep the sales funnel full. However, a major oversight of many salespeople is that they ignore an emptying funnel. They become so focused and excited about developing new leads they fail to remain focused on their commitment to ongoing prospecting. It's not long before they realize their funnel is empty and panic sets in. This could be disastrous as it may be weeks or months before another potential customer works through the funnel. Be cognizant of your funnel inventory and continue to fill it with new opportunities, all while servicing and growing existing accounts.

As a sales entrepreneur, you must actively pursue new potential accounts to ensure you meet and exceed your sales and personal goals. With a customer attrition rate of approximately 15–30% and the constant threat of local and global competition, you can't afford to ignore the significant contribution prospecting makes to a business. Without a commitment to growth, how do you expect to meet or exceed those new quota targets assigned to you every year? You won't. Remember, employers reward results, not activities.

Speaking of growth, it's important that as a sales entrepreneur, you understand the difference between economic growth and real growth.

Growth Versus Real Growth

Time for a quick lesson in sales economics 101. Very few salespeople, management included, appreciate the difference between economic growth and real growth. I bring this concept forward because I have seen many salespeople and sales managers base performance appraisals and productivity on the wrong indicator. *Growth* is a result of a strong, buoyant economy; growth due to outside factors such as low interest rates, high consumer confidence, high demand, and limited supply. Your business becomes the beneficiary of economic growth stimulated by a strong, active economy. You did nothing to stimulate it—you only *reacted* to it. This scenario often creates a false sense of productivity throughout the company as management proudly high-fives each other. In boardrooms, they exclaim: "Aren't we great, we are 15% ahead of last year's numbers. Wow, we're awesome." Who's kidding whom? Yes, you may be up 15% but so is everybody else in your industry. You're all on the bandwagon together, riding on the coattails of strong economic growth. However, *real growth* is over and above economic growth—growth on top of growth. Real growth is stimulated by effective prospecting and is critical for long-term success. For example, if the economy generates 15% economic growth, your goal may be to achieve 5% real growth in addition to the 15%. Thus, when the economic wave crashes (they usually do) and the 15% growth evaporates, you're still left with 5% growth— probably 5% more than your competitors. That's *real* growth. It doesn't take very long to see and appreciate the tremendous impact real growth has on a business. Salespeople and managers usually don't think about growth in these terms. It's time you did. Reevaluate your productivity and challenge yourself. Is my business growing, or is it *really* growing? Clearly, your objective as a sales entrepreneur is to drive real growth. Don't simply respond to a natural economic growth spurt.

Where to Find Them: 22 Ideas

With that end in mind, I offer you the following 22 prospecting sources to help stimulate real growth within your territory and your business—ME INC.

1. **Newspapers.** Review the business section, want ads, and business articles to get company names and ideas as to whom you might want to approach. Look for corporate announcements as well. The newspaper can provide lots of ideas.

2. **Industry Associations.** Get a listing of companies and individuals who belong to specific associations—legal, medical, engineering, and so on. Consider offering yourself as a keynote speaker at their next meeting. They are always looking for ways to spice up their meetings—maybe you're the answer. If you are terrified of speaking to a group, bring along someone from your company who enjoys it. Your company will look good and you'll get the leads.

3. **Yellow Pages.** This is an excellent source of businesses within your territory. Start calling from the back of the book with the Zs and work forward. Most salespeople start at A and never get past the Es. Chances are good that businesses toward the back of the book have never been called. You may want to consider purchasing Yellow Pages from other cities that are within your geographical territory. Alternatively, you can access Yellow Pages for any city on the Internet.

4. **Vehicles on the Road.** Get company names and phone numbers painted on the hundreds of trucks, service vehicles, and company vans you see every day. They may even have a toll-free number proudly displayed, so use your handy tape recorder to record the information. Then follow up.

5. **Trade Shows.** You can't get a faster introduction to a large number of customers all under one roof. I have met some of my largest customers at trade shows. However, don't be intrusive and try to sell them at the show. Rather, ask a few up-front questions to determine their potential then get a name to follow up with later. Call your local convention center or chamber of commerce and get a calendar of upcoming events.

6. **Library.** Use your local library. It often has current business publications, annual reports, and an archive of newspaper

articles on micro-fiche. Make a copy of relevant articles, announcements, and want ads. Then put them in your prospecting file for future follow-up.

7. **The Internet.** The world's largest library is at your fingertips. If it's not on the Net, it hasn't been thought of or invented yet. Use it to retrieve valuable information about a specific industry, investigate new technologies related to your field, subscribe to mailing lists, tap into a newsgroup, and so on. The Internet offers a plethora of opportunities for prospecting and sources of information otherwise unavailable to you. However, I caution you: It can be time-consuming. Don't become a mouse potato and waste away selling hours or janitorial hours distracted by the fun of it.

8. **Friends and Allies.** Ask among your circle of friends and current business allies for referrals. They are often willing to help you out—simply for the price of asking. After all, the more people you know, the more people you're capable of knowing. As one of my friends said, "It's not who you know, it's who I know."

9. **Breakfast Clubs.** Consider joining one that helps you network. They are always looking for new blood, new members. Alternatively, offer yourself as a speaker—they often look for interesting people to feature as a keynote. Talk about an exciting, interesting new technology developed by your company or emerging trends within your industry. Heck, you'll probably get a free breakfast out of it and it's a great way to get your day started.

10. **Old Files.** Take a gander through old files in the office. I'm sure you'll find some orphan accounts—perhaps even some potential born-again accounts.

11. **Target Markets.** Pursue a specific profession and learn what you can about it. For example, it might be legal, medical,

communication, transportation, construction, food service, and so on. However, don't try to spread yourself too thin. Concentrate on one or two specific professions and become an expert in that field.

12. **Subscriptions.** Subscribe to appropriate business magazines. They are often rich with corporate articles and advertisements that may introduce you to the new kid on the block or to a company you haven't heard of before.

13. **Referrals.** Perhaps the most overlooked source for new business. Simply ask existing customers for a couple of names that they would be comfortable passing along. There are plenty of books and seminars outlining effective strategies of networking. I suggest you consider honing your networking skills because the return on your investment is like no other.

14. **Business Directories.** Several companies offer business directories that list all the businesses in your area. Listings include size, locations, president's name, executives, revenue, product lines, and key contacts. These directories can be purchased for a nominal fee and can be broken down by geographical area, revenue, size, or by number of employees. Some directories have the option of cross-referencing phone numbers, addresses, subsidiaries, and parent companies. It can be a worthwhile investment.

15. **Internal Customers.** Nonsales employees can be encouraged to provide leads. An uncle, cousin, or a friend who works at a company might be a potential customer. Even the people in the service department could be very helpful to you. Some companies support this method by offering a financial incentive for every prospective customer they pass along. If the company doesn't pay an incentive consider offering one yourself—even if it's only a $50 gift certificate

for a local restaurant. People generally respond favorably to gestures of appreciation.

16. **Observation.** Keep your eyes and ears open. We are bombarded daily with thousands of messages—billboards, radio, advertisements, banners, TV, and so on. Look for anything new within or around your territory—construction, an information sign on a building, or remodelling in progress. Take an unfamiliar route to your existing customer to see what's going on in and around your territory. Don't drive by and wonder—stop in and find out.

17. **Building Directories.** Every office building has a directory on the main floor that lists the businesses throughout the building. I used to take a picture of it or recite the names into my tape recorder then follow up by telephone and qualify for any possible potential customers.

18. **Social Contacts.** This goes beyond your immediate circle of friends and family to include neighbors, members of social, community and religious organizations; former classmates and any other group whose members might buy the type of product or service that you offer. These social events are an opportunity to meet new and interesting people. However, be tactful when pursuing these contacts. Don't come across as the leech who's always looking for a lead—who looks at every social event as a potential sale. Simply have an informal business chat and agree to follow up during regular business hours or when it's convenient.

19. **Existing Accounts.** Look for additional opportunities within your active accounts. We can get very complacent working with only one department or one division, sometimes overlooking other opportunities that are right under our nose. Ask for a current organizational chart and prospect the entire company—take your blinders off.

20. **Acquisitions and Mergers.** Read the business section of your local newspaper and watch for any announcements of acquisitions and/or mergers. Your favorite account could triple in size overnight and open up an opportunity to pursue new business—real growth. Armed with an endorsement as an incumbent, your chances of success within the new company are excellent.

21. **Social Clubs.** Consider joining a social club or a service club such as a Rotary Club, Lions Club, or The Chamber of Commerce. It not only gives you an opportunity to volunteer for a worthy cause, it is a great avenue for networking.

22. **Cold Calling.** I have saved the best for last. The dreaded cold call! The very thought of it sets in motion all sorts of immobilizing defence mechanisms and excuses. Most salespeople have somehow convinced themselves that cold calling is unprofessional, intrusive, and unnecessary. I hear them say: "We don't make cold calls in our business. We get leads from referrals, tradeshows, ads, and our regular customers." That's all fine and good but don't be too quick to abdicate—very few businesses are immune to the benefits of cold calling. It is the backbone of good prospecting and when done properly it will yield high potential prospects. Cold calling can be a very lucrative part of your sales strategy.

Professional Cold Calling

By definition, a cold call is where you know absolutely nothing about a particular account and you drop in unannounced to qualify them. You have never made a visit to that account before. The only familiarity lies in the fact you have been driving past it for a year.

Often a lack of cold-calling confidence, driven by fear, sabotages the best intentions. Overcoming that fear begins with an effective, professional cold-calling strategy. Most authors would agree that cold calling in itself is not unprofessional, but the approach has tarnished its reputation. Nowhere is it written that cold calling is taboo. In fact, without cold calling, your customer base is not as rich and varied and you seriously jeopardize real growth and the success of your business. The reality is that *fear* is the biggest barrier to an effective cold calling campaign. Fear of rejection, embarrassment, and feeling awkward in a strange environment. It's much easier to pursue the *comfortable* route and have businesses come in by other means rather than expose yourself to the possible perils of cold calling.

You can no longer afford to deny yourself or your business the tremendous benefits of cold calling. To that end, I offer you the following three steps as a guideline to making professional, results-oriented cold calls. This approach may not be applicable in all situations so massage it to fit your sales arena. By the way, one big plus of cold calling is that you'll never be late.

1. **Introduction.** When you arrive, introduce yourself to the receptionist using these four components, in order: 1) your name, 2) your company name, 3) what you do, and 4) that

you are cold calling. Don't try to skirt the issue, tell the receptionist up-front that you are cold calling. Next step is to ask them for their help. Most of the time they will be quite receptive to helping. Gatekeepers see a lot of salespeople come and go throughout the day so be sure your approach is professional, friendly, and respectful. Heck, the absolute worst thing that can happen is they ask you to leave. That's OK—next.

2. **Planning.** Because it's a cold call you know nothing, or very little, about this business, so do some homework. First, ask the receptionist for her help. "Would you mind helping me out by answering a few questions?" In most cases she will oblige. Second, ask her for a corporate package; i.e., annual report, company brochures, newsletters, anything that will help you better understand the business. Refer to Chapter 3 for more detailed information that may be helpful with your cold-call planning and preparation. Take some time in the lobby to review the material. Don't leave yet.

3. **Announce Yourself.** Now it's time to announce yourself but be sure it's to the right person. Throughout your planning, you have learned that Bert is the manager and he may be your contact. However, it's not Bert you want to see, at least not yet. Ask who Bert's boss is and announce yourself to that person. Go at least one level up, to Susan. Follow the theory that it's easier to work downhill than uphill. Pick up the phone in the lobby, or use your cell phone and call Susan directly. Why have a busy, overworked gatekeeper announce you. Announce yourself. Who is better suited to introduce yourself than you!

When she answers, you need to restate the four components of your introduction, including the fact that you are cold calling. (I have found many executives are impressed when you tell them that you are in their lobby making a cold call.) After your introduction be sure to say this: "Susan, I realize you generally work with appointments and that I am unannounced, but would you have a second to exchange business cards?" It's very important to acknowledge that you are unannounced and without an appointment. That's what makes your cold call professional and different from the others. Also, by asking to "exchange business cards," Susan will associate that with a shorter time period than if you had asked, "Do you have a minute?" The other advantage is that it attaches a purpose to your introduction whereas, "Got a minute?" is somewhat ambiguous. If Susan comes out to meet you, offer your business card and again acknowledge that you are unannounced, without an appointment. If Susan declines your request to meet in the lobby, ask her when she is available and use your time management system to book an appointment.

Now that you have met Susan and exchanged pleasantries, (use PSIP—Chapter 7—to guide your conversation) ask her if she has a couple minutes to answer a few quick questions. If she says yes, take advantage of this opportunity and ask questions to further qualify the account and also identify who the decision maker is (who is the bag of money?). However, your first question should be, "How much time do I have?" Show respect for her time. After all, you are unannounced. During your conversation ask Susan these five questions:

1. Does Bert make the decisions?

2. Does Bert have a budget?

3. Will Bert talk to you prior to a decision?

4   Will you introduce me to Bert?

5. If Bert approves of our proposal may I accompany Bert when he presents to you?

If the answer is "yes" to #3, you know Susan makes the decisions, not Bert. However, you will have to respect Bert's position and sell him on your proposal. Otherwise, it will never go any further.

Question #4 is what I refer to as corporate cascading. Susan introducing you to Bert. Powerful stuff. Because your introduction to Bert was through Susan, Bert will be receptive to meet you. Bert won't be upset with you for going over his head because you have never met him before. He can only be curious as to your approach.

If Susan is not in the office or is unavailable, try to meet briefly with her executive assistant. Assistants can be informative and helpful. They may also book appointments for Susan. If not, ask her to check with Susan for available meeting times.

The Susan/Bert strategy is a very effective approach to cold calling. I have used it successfully for years. Rather than do a typical cold call where you leave a business card and a brochure and depart empty-handed, consider implementing the Susan/Bert strategy.

However, before you throw this book down and protest your resistance to cold calling, you don't have to do it all the time. I'm not suggesting that cold calling become your *modus operandi,* but it can be very effective at appropriate times. The two best times are to fill in blank time caused by cancelled appointments, or to plan a half day in a certain area of your territory to cold call. For example, upon learning that your 10 AM appointment was cancelled, don't go back to the adult daycare center, go cold calling and make productive use of the time before your next appointment. My informal research suggests that 50% of the time you cold call, you find at least one new potential account. As Woody Allen says, "80% of life is showing up."

Although prospecting is the lifeblood to any successful business, it remains one of the most feared and avoided activities of selling. Overcoming reluctance to prospecting means developing a plan, setting goals, and keeping good records. To help build your confidence, you may want to consider doing a "ride-along" with an experienced sales entrepreneur who is good at prospecting. Tag along for the afternoon and simply observe how it's done. Observation is a powerful learning tool.

As you build your confidence, experiment with different methods and ideas to find the prospecting combination that works well for you and your business. There is no single universal method, no optimal mode to fit all situations. Your prospect-

ing strategies need to be situational to your sales arena, maximizing your ROT (return on time equity). I don't suggest that all 22 ideas will work for you but do concentrate on developing a combination of methods and you will see it stimulate your business and drive *real* growth. Become an expert in the methods that have the greatest impact on your productivity.

Congratulations, you have now completed
Step #3

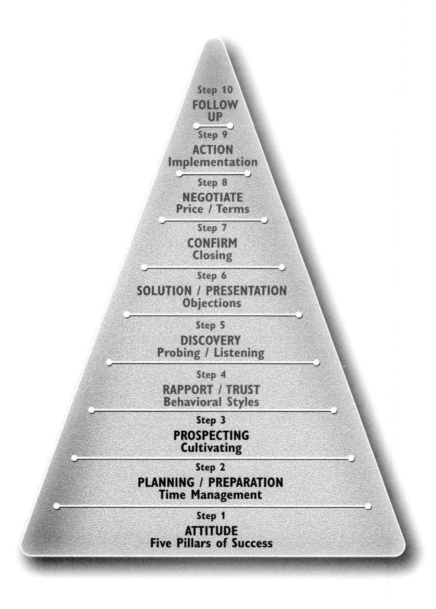

Chapter 6

BUILDING RAPPORT AND TRUST:
BEHAVIORAL FLEXIBILITY

Behavioral flexibility is proving to be one of the most useful tools you can add to your intellectual inventory, your professional equity. Understanding style types and learning how to adjust (not change) your approach fosters rapport and trust with your customer, while helping meet and exceed your customer's communication expectations. Sales entrepreneurs understand that the full dynamics of interpersonal communication go beyond the basic communication model of sender (encoding) and receiver (decoding).

Different customers require different selling approaches. Behavioral flexibility provides a tool for us to adapt to different selling situations. Its application continues to grow in popularity as business people learn to appreciate the tremendously positive impact behavioral flexibility has on relationships.

Building and maintaining rapport and trust are the cornerstones to any relationship. So what's the difference between rapport and trust? Rapport can be instantaneous or developed in a very short period of time. It means having something in common with the party you are meeting. Part of forming a first impression is deciding whether you like this person enough to continue the conversation without barriers. Sometimes when you meet someone new, you instantly feel good about him or her. Rapport develops quickly. Perhaps it's like the "love at first sight" feeling. Trust takes longer. Trust is developed over time and is based on honesty, consistency, integrity, and professionalism. It's following through on your commitments and promises. I may initially like you (rapport) but it may take a bit of time before I trust you. Thus, rapport and trust must work in accord for the relationship to advance. These are two common denominators to any endeavor in life and to any relationship, including relations with your internal customers, kids, siblings, and spouse.

The pioneer who developed the psychology of style types was a Swiss psychologist, Dr. Carl Jung. He initially observed differences in his parents' behavioral styles and his fascination led to years of studying the differences among people. He began his research in the late 1800s and in 1921 he wrote *Psychology Types*. Jung's research eventually revealed four basic behavioral types: Initiator, Thinker, Feeler, and Sensor. Most of his work focuses on internal characteristics that lead to external behaviors. Another point to consider: It is suggested that you are born with a predominate style that does not change as you go through life. Once a thinker, always a thinker. That's not to say you don't experience traits from the other styles; you do. Jung's work simply suggests that you have a primary personality style. The four styles I refer to later in this chapter are Socializer, Director, Thinker, and Relater, all evolving from Carl Jung's work.

How Do I Get Them to Like Me?

Behavioral adaptability is the key to successful application of the behavioral flexibility model. Adaptability means you have the maturity and confidence to behave in a style that may not be your primary style, but that reflects the style of your customer. Sales entrepreneurs consciously go out of their comfort zone in order to establish a relationship of rapport and trust.

By recognizing the styles of yourself and others, you can adapt your behavior to fit the situation. Adapting speeds up the *likeable* factor. People are naturally drawn to like-minded people with similar styles. If you can embrace and parallel the behavioral style of your customers, they can't help but appreciate your approach and, consciously or unconsciously, begin to like you. In their book, *The Art of Speedreading People,* Paul and Barbara Tieger talk about the tremendous sales advantage of speedreading your customers—identifying the customer's style type and adapting. They go on to suggest that your next goal is to *speed-reach* your customer—communicate on the customer's own level based on the style type you have identified. You need to observe and listen carefully to your customer and respond in the way that best accommodates his or her behavioral type.

Developing your skill in reading and interpreting people's behavioral style helps manage the initial tension that exists in any new relationship. As Tony Alessandra says in his book, *People Smarts,* "You can learn to adapt your style to handle different types of situations, even the more difficult ones that we encounter in the real-world laboratory of life." He goes on to suggest this tool is not about changing, it's about acting in a "sensible, successful way" to nurture a lasting relationship. Perhaps Dr. Richard Carlson says it most succinctly in his book, *Don't Sweat the Small Stuff . . . and it's all small stuff:*

> For many people, one of the most frustrating aspects of life is not being able to understand other people's behavior. We see them as "guilty" instead of "innocent." It's tempting to focus on people's seemingly irrational behavior—their comments, actions, mean-spirited acts, selfish behavior—and get extremely frustrated. If we focus on behavior too much, it can seem like other people are making us miserable. It's true that other people do weird things (who doesn't?), but we are the ones getting upset, so we are the ones who need to change.

I'm merely talking about learning to be less bothered by the actions of people.

Carlson goes on to suggest that, "When someone is acting in a way we don't like, the best strategy for dealing with that person is to look *beyond* it and see the innocence in where the behavior is coming from."

Parallel to Carlson's thinking, I offer this explanation of behavioral flexibility: An understanding of the behavior model gives us the patience to tolerate other people and their actions—including internal customers such as spouse, kids, and family. You can't change your style or other people's styles, but you can change the relationship.

Four Behavioral Styles of Customers

The following style grid outlines the four styles and positions them in relation to the vertical and horizontal axis.

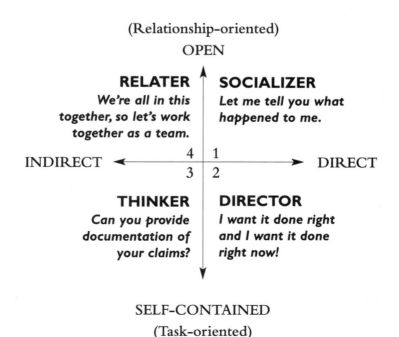

The vertical axis is the *openness* scale, which refers to how willing the person is to be open and to reveal what is happening on the inside. At the top, we have highly open, talkative, friendly, relationship-oriented individuals: *extroverts*. At the bottom, we find self-contained, quiet, very closed individuals: *introverts*. The introverts are self-contained people, usually expressionless, not revealing their feelings, thoughts, or emotions. Their world is internal and it can be difficult to read them or know what they're thinking. Comparatively, the extroverts readily show excitement, joy, enthusiasm, anger, and a variety of emotions.

The horizontal axis is referred to as the *directness* scale: direct or indirect. People who are direct, on the right side, make decisions quickly and easily: not a lot of details are required. These people are spontaneous, "Sure, sounds good, let's do it." Their motto is, "It's easier to get forgiveness than permission." People who are indirect, on the left side, are not as comfortable making quick decisions. They move more cautiously, arriving at a decision more slowly. A direct individual may very well get frustrated by the amount of time an indirect person takes to make a decision. Conversely, an indirect person is not impressed with how quickly and recklessly a direct person makes decisions. It's all about understanding that people are different. Your interactions with people succeed when you heed their external signals. Interactions fail when you ignore the signals. Now for the bad news and good news: the bad news is there is only one thing you can control and change; the good news is, it's you. Don't try to change other people; you can't. The high divorce rate proves it. Even marriage counselors are in agreement that the behavioral flexibility model goes a long way toward improving relationships. The following pages outline the primary characteristics of each style. Let's have a look at each style and as you read through them, try to ascertain the style that best fits your behavior, at work and at home.

Socializer

These are fun-loving extroverts, social people who are full of life and always appear to be enjoying themselves, having fun. Their preference is *party first, business second*. The best way to get their attention and build rapport is to have fun with them before you get down to business. They are energetic, enthusiastic, talkative, and literally the life of any party. They are sharp dressers, very stylish, and sometimes outrageous. Socializers are not afraid of drawing attention to themselves; in fact, they prefer it. They love toys and often drive high-end sports cars: red Porsches, Lamborghinis, or Dodge Stealths. They also have all the accessories: jewelry, expensive watches, shoes, pens, etc. A $1,000 outfit with all the trimmings is not uncommon.

The downside about Socializers is that they are poor listeners and inattentive, since they are usually focused on talking about themselves. It's sometimes tough to get a word in edgewise as they tell you their life stories and fondest dreams. Nevertheless, you must give them time to chat and party with you before asking business questions.

A word of caution: Socializers hate detail and boring, lengthy presentations. They can be very impatient. Make it fun, colorful, exciting, and get to the bottom line quickly. Sell the sizzle more than the steak. Bottom line to a Socializer means, "How will this make me look good and will it be fun?" Get the deal in writing. Socializers tend to forget quickly as they move on to the next event or party. The best vehicle to build trust and rapport is to put fun into the relationship. Energize your call with enthusiasm and excitement. After all, if you have fun socializing and pass the party test by listening to the jokes and stories, then it only stands to reason that you will be a trustworthy, enjoyable person to do business with. The big plus is that they will, and do, make quick decisions (direct) as you move through the steps of your Sequential Model. In summary:

SOCIALIZER

Open/
Relationship-oriented

- *Extroverted, assertive*
- *Party first, business second*
- *Very talkative, lots of stories and jokes*
- *Very friendly, approachable, likes fun people*
- *Flashy, sharp dresser, stylish*
- *Enthusiastic, lots of energy*
- *Quick decisions, spontaneous*
- *Poor listener*
- *Very ME oriented*
- *Hates detail, wants big picture*
- *Hates routine, rules, lineups*
- *Comfortable, warm office, leather couch*
- *Confirm the sale with excitement and enthusiasm*

Direct/
Spontaneous

Director

Here is your consummate businessperson, an introvert whose main focus is the task at hand and who is guided by goals and objectives. Directors are always asking, "What's the point?" Thus, it's always *business first, party maybe*. Get to the point quickly and don't socialize or try to encourage social conversation. They will become impatient and tune out quickly as they are simply not interested. Directors love control and prefer to be in charge; they like being the boss. As an introvert, they have a low tolerance for feelings and emotions. Directors can appear to be quiet, unfriendly, and apathetic. Directors are quite happy to do things on their own—see a movie, dine in a restaurant, or even travel. They will tell you, "I'm alone, but not lonely."

Directors often prefer to give cash or gift certificates as gifts rather than take the time to shop. Their dress is usually dark blue and conservative, nothing flashy or terribly stylish. If a Director is wearing a flashy tie you can feel safe in asking, "Nice tie, who

I think we are just about out of time. Can you leave me a brochure?

bought it for you?" They drive conservative, functional cars such as a Reliant or a Taurus. Don't touch a Director, in fact, handshakes are unnecessary. They like their personal space, "We are here to do business, not get married!" A Director is not concerned about the relationship, they just care about your performance as a professional and how the performance of your product or service will contribute to the bottom line. Don't have an emotional outburst (crying) in a Director's office. He or she will be unmoved and unimpressed. Get yourself together—then carry on with the conversation. No sniffling allowed. Remember, Directors have a need for power and control that cannot be ignored by a pushy sales representative. They are motivated by bottom-line detail. In summary:

DIRECTOR

Direct/Spontaneous

- *Introverted, shows little emotion*
- *Business first, maybe party*
- *Always asking: what's the point?*
- *Get to the point quickly, no socializing*
- *Focused on goals, objectives and getting the task done*
- *Conservative dresser, nothing flashy*
- *Handshakes are unnecessary*
- *Wants bottom-line detail, avoid the feature dump*
- *Fast decisions, spontaneous*
- *Cash or gift certificates as gifts, hates shopping*
- *Poor listener*
- *Needs to be in CONTROL, in charge*
- *Very plain office, clean desk, nothing on walls*
- *Confirm the sale with bottom-line detail*

Self-Contained/
Task-oriented

Thinker

The two main components of a Thinker are indirect (slow decisions) and self-contained (introvert). These individuals are typically your engineers, accountants, and computer programmers. It's *information first, then business.* You don't have much hope of doing business with them until you deliver all the required data for them to make an informed, intelligent decision. Thinkers hate to be wrong—it drives them crazy when mistakes are made. That's why they are indirect, not making decisions quickly, avoiding mistakes. They are very detailed-oriented and precise, often guided by the letter of the law, versus the spirit of the law. Presentations to Thinkers must be logical, accurate, and reliable. Thinkers are the ones who will lure you into a feature dump. They love it. Rather than spewing reams of information, ask them what *they* would like to see. They will tell you what's important to them so make sure you provide it. I suggest you openly acknowledge their need for information, then ask, "What specific information would you need to see to build your

I have to go. Another sales rep just showed up with very important information.

confidence to buy from me?" Build confidence by presenting appropriate information guided by the Thinkers' feedback. Dumping wheelbarrels of data in their office for their perusal only lengthens the sales cycle. Edit your dialogue with data that are relevant and appropriate to the Thinker.

Expect Thinkers to compare your product or service to the competition. Seldom will they accept information at face value. Impulse buying is very uncomfortable for them. They prefer to research manufacturer's specifications and converse with experts in that field. Don't argue with them; there isn't much chance of winning. Why? Because they have thoroughly researched the subject and have the data to back themselves up, and they will pursue the argument until they are victorious. In some cases Thinkers' attitudes are: "I'm right and you're wrong but it's your right to be wrong."

Of the four styles, Thinkers are the ones least concerned with dress—it's not important. Their clothes are a bit worn and generally a bit out of style. They sometimes wear a plastic pocket protector full of Bic pens and use duct tape to fix their glasses. I know some Thinkers who insist on hanging toilet paper "correctly," exercising proper toilet paper management, so that it rolls off the top. This is an important detail to Thinkers and in fact, they have been known to correct it when they get home. They sometimes even correct it at a friend's home, just to help out. It has been the topic of many heated matrimonial discussions. Of course the Directors are thinking: "Who cares? I'm happy if there's paper on the back of the toilet."

Thinkers tend to be packrats, never throwing anything out. Their garages and basements are jammed with old stuff because, "You just never know when it might be useful." Heck, they even have their university text books and notes somewhere in the basement.

Thinkers focus on two important aspects of selling: accuracy and an eye to detail. They are particular on their paperwork, which is appreciated by internal customers. They tend to do a job right the first time, whereas Socializers may have to redo it several times as they often overlook important details. In summary:

THINKER

Indirect ⟵─────────────────────────────────

- *Introverted, analytical*
- *Detail first, then business*
- *Detail oriented, needs to be accurate*
- *Provides lots of facts and data*
- *Loves the feature dump*
- *Not a great dresser, conservative*
- *Slow decisions, must be CORRECT*
- *Constantly asking questions*
- *Embarrassed when wrong*
- *Not spontaneous, hates surprises*
- *Hangs toilet paper correctly*
- *Hard to change their mind*
- *Very loyal once commitment is made*
- *Confirm by presenting appropriate information*

Self-Contained/
Task-oriented

Relater

The two main components of a Relater are indirect (slow decisions) and open (extrovert). These individuals are very sensitive, often taking business issues personally. They are very intuitive, accurately reading people's nonverbal behaviors. Relaters are big-time team players and they encourage harmony among the

Wow, that's awesome. I sure appreciate the invitation.

team, be it at work, socially, or at home with their family. Relaters are emotional, empathetic people who are moved to tears easily and can be oversensitive. Take a Relater to see *Titanic* and watch what happens. They cry very easily. (Yes, even male Relaters.) Directors would be inclined to think, "Why are you crying, you knew the darn thing sank in 1912." Relaters are often appalled at the apparent apathy of Directors, taking their verbal and nonverbal responses literally. Relaters hate conflict of any sort. They go to great lengths to avoid hassles, talking their way out of conflict. They are very conforming and go with the flow versus doing it solo. Relaters are good listeners and ask more than tell. Relaters are motivated by the relationship, hoping everybody will like them. They must be popular and tend to make decisions slowly (indirect) so as to not offend or upset anyone with an unpopular decision. When shopping, Relaters will often ask, "What's popular, what's selling?" The use of references is very effective with Relaters—they build confidence in your product or service. Relaters like to be assured that they are not the only ones using your product or service. Your proposal must support or enhance the people side of the business, concentrating on harmony, security, and concrete benefits. Ask them frequently about their opinions and ideas. In summary:

RELATER

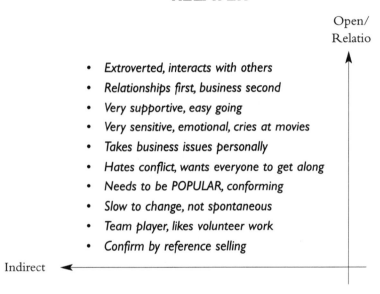

Open/
Relatio

- *Extroverted, interacts with others*
- *Relationships first, business second*
- *Very supportive, easy going*
- *Very sensitive, emotional, cries at movies*
- *Takes business issues personally*
- *Hates conflict, wants everyone to get along*
- *Needs to be POPULAR, conforming*
- *Slow to change, not spontaneous*
- *Team player, likes volunteer work*
- *Confirm by reference selling*

Indirect

How Will I Know When I See One?

There are two primary indicators of one's style, verbal and visual. As Tony Alessandra suggests, there are "observable characteristics" for each style—visual indicators such as environment, dress, vehicle, office, and how each verbalizes thoughts and ideas. As well, be cognizant of nonverbal gestures. By observing how customers dress and express themselves, and by listening to how and what they say, you will quickly begin to identify their styles. I suggest you begin by asking yourself, "Is he or she an introvert or an extrovert?" These traits can be rather obvious in their approach, dress, and work environment. Look around their corporate livingroom (office) and observe what is and isn't there, including pictures, awards, certificates, type of furniture, toys, bric-a-brac, and so on. Then narrow it down to a particular quadrant, keeping in mind that each individual exhibits characteristics and behaviors from each quadrant. People are not restricted to the conduct associated with just one style.

Different Versus Difficult

Know the difference between different and difficult. Unfortunately, it seems that few people do. We are often too quick to label someone as "difficult" when they act or behave in a manner contrary to our behavior. You see, people are not difficult, they are just different. It's far too easy to label them as difficult, rather than make the effort to understand them and appreciate their differences. That's what makes this tool such an asset to your professional equity. Understand that people—your customers—are different. The key to a lasting, trusting relationship is an adaptation to *their* style. Abraham Lincoln once said, "I don't like that man very much; I need to get to know him better." What a great concept, one from which we could all benefit.

As a new salesperson with a company, you may have heard (or even said) this: "Don't bother going to see Hank at XYZ Company. He is such a jerk and a real tough guy to get along with. Plus, he never buys anything—he's always just looking." Hank may very well be a jerk (they do exist) but chances are that Hank is simply a different style type. Hank is probably a neat guy once you get to know him. A case in point: I recently received a call from an excited graduate of my sales program. She was ecstatic because she had just confirmed business with an account that had been labelled indifferent and not likely to buy from her. She persevered, and with the help of behavioral flexibility she secured a $100,000 account. Not a bad return on her training investment.

Another important aspect of successful adaptation is your willingness and confidence to stretch your comfort zone. As discussed in Chapter 2, stretching your comfort zone is one of the pillars of success, and is certainly a necessary attitude for successful implementation of behavioral flexibility. We must be willing and able to stretch our range to accommodate other people's styles.

So who makes the best salesperson? Before I answer this common question, put the book down and give it some thought. I'll wait.

The answer is . . . the chameleon—the salesperson who can readily adapt to the style of each customer. It doesn't matter which style you are. What matters is how quickly and comfortably you can adapt to the style of the person you are interacting with, at home or at work.

General Observations

At this point you are probably getting a good appreciation for differences among the four behavioral styles. To further crystallize your understanding, I offer these real-world, everyday scenarios:

Reading a Newspaper

- Socializers look for stories about the party they were at the previous night. They do things that get themselves *in* the paper. They scan the entire paper looking for interesting, current-event articles. They read the Entertainment section.

- Directors mainly read the headlines and the business section. They then turn to the sports section to read about athletic accomplishments.

- Thinkers call the newspaper if a word is incorrectly spelled or a story is inaccurate.

- Relaters look for a popular, current event story to discuss at the office water cooler. They check the obituaries to see if they know anyone.

Golfing

- Socializers spend more time in the clubhouse talking and welcoming new members. Their "almost a hole in one" story is repeated frequently for the benefit of new members.

- Directors drive the cart and frequently try to play through.

- Thinkers keep score for the group and often refer to the rule book. They keep their clubs clean too.

- Relaters play regularly with the same foursome, usually offering to buy the beverages at the 19th hole.

Grocery Shopping

- Socializers approach the "fewer than 9 items" checkout line, begin a conversation and compare the fun stuff in other shopping carts. They hold up the line by conversing with the cashier about upcoming holidays.

- Directors approach and barrel through the "fewer than 9 items" line with 15 items. After all, it was the shortest line.

- Thinkers approach the same checkout line wrestling with the correct thing to do. "Are the eggs one item, or 12?" They also count items in other carts and if they are over the limit, they become irritated.

- Relaters approach the "fewer than 9 items" line, count the items, and take comfort knowing they have only eight. If they have ten items, they move to another line.

The Desk

- Socializers say: "I'm busy right now. Give me a few minutes and I'll get back to you." They don't know where the item is on their desk, but won't admit it.

- Directors have a clean desk, one file out at a time. Nothing else is on the desk. Even their telephone is on the credenza behind them.

- Thinkers say, "It's the third report down in that pile." The desk is messy, with Post-It-Notes and files everywhere, but they know exactly where everything is.

- Relaters have everything in place, with the most impressive, business-related file in full view. A family picture and a picture of him or her shaking hands with a celebrity is in a prominent position. Relaters have a separate table for visitors rather than sitting at their desk.

Cooking

- Socializers like to cook for groups. They prepare an extra place at the table just in case company stops by. They go out rather than cook for one.

- Directors can't cook without a microwave. They buy single portions. Cooking is viewed as a functional necessity versus a social event.

- Thinkers cook with a cookbook, a timer, and a measuring cup. Directions are followed exactly, with no deviations allowed.

- Relaters like to prepare a meal from scratch using a dozen standard recipes, taking the best from each and using the most popular ingredients.

Elevators

- Socializers let everyone in, saying, "Always room for one more, the more the merrier." They ignore the "max limit" sign and hand out business cards on the way down.

- Directors walk up, push the button, wait impatiently, get in and speak to no one. If running late, they take the stairs.

- Thinkers enter, but if it's crowded they count the number of people. If over the limit, they will ask someone to leave.

- Relaters hold the door for others and ensure they're the last ones on, in case it's full. They don't want to crowd anybody. If so, they will wait for the next elevator. They smile at everyone on the trip down.

The development of any new skill takes practice, and lots of it. The first step requires your personal commitment to this challenge and belief in the behavioral flexibility principles. I strongly encourage you to accept this opportunity to strengthen your relationship competencies and develop your interpersonal skills. Let's face it, you and your customer become the beneficiaries.

I suggest you practice by identifying the styles among members of your family, coworkers, and friends. At your next social event, sit back and consciously observe people, their dress, their actions, how and with whom they converse, and so on. You'll be amazed at how much behavioral flexibility is real world and how people quickly reveal their predominant style.

As a guideline to practice, ask yourself these questions:

- Are they introvert or extrovert?

- Do they appear to be direct or indirect?

- How are they dressed?

- What is their predominant quadrant?

Remember, there is nothing mysterious about behavioral flexibility. It's about treating people the way *they* want to be treated. Everybody is different and no two customers are the same. Whether the person is dominant or shy, you will have the confidence and specific strategies for dealing successfully with that individual. Remember, people are not difficult—just different. After all, variety is the spice of . . . sales! A footnote: Don't consider this chapter as your only resource to develop your behavioral flexibility skills. There are many good publications dedicated to the subject and I suggest you consider building your own library on this subject. See the bibliography.

Congratulations, you have now completed
Step #4

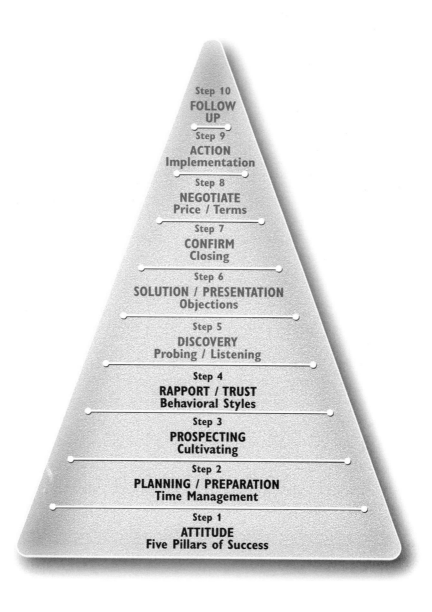

Chapter 7

DISCOVERY: GAME DAY

The starter's pistol has sounded and now is the moment of truth, the opportunity to capitalize on all your preparatory efforts. As you sit face-to-face with your customer, a gold-medal performance is your only option. The sales arena presents no silver or bronze medals, nor does it allow any false starts. On game day, Steps #1 through #4 of your Sequential Model are critical prerequisites to a stellar performance. Chances are your competitor is in the same arena, running the same race, just on a different day.

Your challenge is to move the customer from a cold, indifferent frame of mind to aroused excitement about you and your product or service. Remember that salespeople are often viewed as an intrusion, an interruption to an already busy day. Unless you can change that basic attitude by reducing the initial tension, you are doomed before you start. The initial moments of a sales call are fraught with uncertainty, and tension must be minimized. However, a certain level of tension is healthy and normal as it motivates you to higher levels of performance. Sales entrepreneurs know how to transform nervous pre-call energy into a winning edge, a confident approach. The winning edge is an attitude of a champion. Small differences in attitude and ability can translate into enormous differences in results. A race horse may win by a nose or a PGA golfer by a single stroke, but their

147

winnings may be twice that of second place. Are they twice as good or talented? Of course not. You and your competitor are both invited by the customer to compete. You are both on the short list, but only one will emerge victorious, often winning only by a nose. In sales, it's not your margin of victory that is important but whether you played the game to win, embracing every possible advantage. Remember, your customer is the ultimate judge of your performance. At the awards ceremony, the gold medal is presented in the form of an order.

Needs Analysis

Customer satisfaction begins with a careful diagnosis of needs and expectations. You must sensitize yourself to your customer's issues and focus on what your customer needs to buy, rather than selling what you need to sell. (One more sale and I win the TV!) Through open and honest conversation you will discover the needs and expectations of your potential customer and begin to formulate a solution that differentiates you from your closest competitor. *Discovery,* then, is asking questions through an exploratory discussion, listening carefully, and aligning your offerings to exceed your customer's expectations.

The key to differentiation is asking intelligent questions, questions your competitors don't ask, or are afraid to pose. Asking intelligent questions is the essence of an effective needs analysis that reveals the specifics about a possible solution. However, asking questions is not an isolated event where you show up to the appointment, introduce yourself, then proceed to inundate your customer with an onslaught of scripted questions. Think of discovery as a dialogue, a conversation between two people, rather than a strategic engagement between a salesperson and a customer. Before a customer will open up and share information that may lead to a sale, you must get acquainted, establish rapport, gain trust, and break through the mental barriers usually associated with first-time sales calls. You must demonstrate a genuine interest in the customer to advance the relationship. Granted, it is not easy to break through initial sales resistance, negative perceptions, and a general attitude of apathy toward salespeople. Meeting a customer for the first time can be a nerve-wracking experience for even a seasoned sales professional. Usually, the first few minutes of a sales call are the most stressful for both the salesperson and the customer. The customer's stress comes in the form of uncertainty about the salesperson's intentions and apprehension about seeing "another sales rep." Sales representatives experience stress because they often rely on little more than their good looks and the gift of the gab to carry them through the call. However, thousands of sales *entrepreneurs* are successful every day, proving that customers are receptive if you demonstrate a genuine interest through an approach that is forged from your knowledge, skills, and confidence.

An effective approach requires a method designed to get the customer's attention and interest quickly, while guiding you through the most sensitive part of the call, the first few minutes. Your greatest ally throughout the call is the after-effect of the positive first impression you made. A favorable first impression usually produces a customer who is willing to participate. Customers put tremendous faith in their perceptions and are quick to prejudge. If you are perceived as professional and effective at the beginning of the call, you will be perceived as effective during the rest of the call. The customer's receptivity to you will be decided within the first minute. You never get a second chance to make a first impression.

The PSIP Method

Let's now explore the PSIP method: Pleasantries, Show-off, Inform, Probe. PSIP represents the four navigational buoys of an effective opening strategy, designed to help you neutralize initial tension and make a smooth transition into the needs analysis stage. All four components of PSIP must work in accord with each other in order to take advantage of this proven approach. A well-executed PSIP strategy is your springboard into a smooth opening and is a great confidence builder early in the call. It is a great way to launch into the heart of the sales call, relax the initial tension, stripping away the *stiffness* of the call. A strong opening strategy arouses the customer's curiosity and respect, often setting the tone for the entire call, including telephone calls.

The PSIP method is not reserved for first-time sales calls only. It also works well with existing customers. Just as the Sequential Model must be applied to every sales situation, PSIP must also be utilized at every sales call, regardless of your customer's tenure.

Pleasantries. Customers form an opinion about you within 15 seconds, even before you speak. They evaluate your posture, dress, hygiene, grooming, and attitude.

Pleasantries include two aspects, visual and verbal. First impressions encompass both aspects, and can be a tremendous asset or a costly liability. Many salespeople make a poor impression without realizing it by overlooking important details such as proper dress, punctuality, grooming, and overall professionalism. You can't afford to let any aspect of your approach, visual or verbal, compromise the impression you communicate to your customer. Be cognizant of the impact of your physical appearance and how it can affect your customer's evaluation of you. Your *visual assets,* how you look to the customer, are something to be proud of. This is an important aspect of nonverbal communication. Show up on time feeling good, looking good, thinking good, and ready to do business. Emulate the attitude of a winner, a champion. Customers want to deal with winners, so look like one. The most important presentation you make is to yourself every morning in the mirror.

Verbal pleasantries means initiating social conversation with the customer using local events, current events, or global events as possible topics of conversation. Take 15 minutes before you leave the house or your hotel and peruse the morning paper, perhaps the business section or the sports section. Be informed. It can be a great ice-breaker and a source of conversation, especially if you're from out of town. During the pleasantries stage try to keep the conversation social. Encourage your customer to respond on a personal level rather than on a formal business level. A short, humorous personal story such as, "You'll never guess what happened to me this morning . . ." identifies you as a real human being. It can do wonders to help people relax.

Another big advantage of the pleasantries stage is the opportunity it provides to identify your customer's behavioral style. Ask yourself, "What quadrant is she in?" and "How do I need to adjust?" The pleasantries stage begins to reveal preferred styles by way of dress and mannerisms. A talkative response or a quick short answer to your questions will tell you a lot about your customer's style. Behavioral styles and behavioral flexibility are discussed in detail throughout Chapter 6.

The key to forging a long-term relationship with your customer is to build rapport by way of adjusting to your customer's preferred behavioral style. By definition, rapport means having something in common, a link, some way to connect with your customer. Use behavioural flexibility, coupled with appropriate social conversation, to build rapport. Don't rely on a picture of a sailboat hanging in the office to stimulate conversation. It can be viewed as a shallow approach to building rapport and I'm sure your customer is sick of talking about it every time a sales representative comes into the office.

Depending upon the customer's style, the pleasantries stage can be as quick as one minute or as long as fifteen minutes. Remember, each call is situational. I caution you to safeguard yourself against conversational drift. Don't let the talkative customer dominate all your time with such topics as religion, capital punishment, or empty chatter that compromises the objective of the pleasantry stage.

During the pleasantry stage you begin to understand your customer's preferred business style, just as the customer will have a good feeling about you and your level of confidence. By the way, my previous point about a customer forming an opinion about you within 15 seconds works both ways. You too begin to form an impression about your customer early and quickly.

The best advice I can offer for the pleasantries stage is to be yourself, guided by a positive attitude and the confidence that comes with effective planning and preparation.

Show-off. The second stage of PSIP is the opportunity to show off your new-found wisdom. Take a subtle approach. By way of conversation and visual evidence (annual reports, brochures) let the customer know you've done your homework. This is the point where social conversation (pleasantries) shifts to business conversation. You have invested some non-selling, janitorial hours in planning and preparing so now it's time to get a return on that investment. Your return comes in the form of the customer's appreciation for your obvious commitment and professionalism. As discussed in Chapter 3, take an, "Oh, by the way" approach to present your information. Take out their annual report and any brochures that you received prior to the call and refer to them. For example, "Oh, by the way, I noticed in your annual report some comments about your recent acquisition of ABC Company," or "I noticed in your brochures you manufacture ten different models." You can even use competitive intelligence to show off by saying, "I understand your competitors have discontinued manufacturing their . . ." This demonstrates your knowledge of their industry as well as their business. Powerful stuff. What better way to get your customers' interest and attention and build credibility than by talking about their business? The examples of show-off items are endless, but be sure to relate your show-off items to current, relevant information about their business.

A case in point: My associate and I made a sales call to the head office of a company. We arrived early for our appointment, and had an opportunity to review some additional literature displayed in their lobby. Our contact, the VP of Quality and Training, introduced himself and showed us into the boardroom. We had barely sat down, working through the pleasantries stage, when he asked us, "What do you know about our company?" With great enthusiasm my associate produced their annual report and a few of their brochures attained prior to the appointment and then proceeded to talk about their business. We had done our homework. The customer was impressed with our knowledge. We had earned the right to proceed with the call and the next hour went very well. His confidence in us led to an introduction to the VP of Sales and Marketing, a pivotal decisionmaker in the sales process.

The show-off stage has tremendous impact on the outcome of your sales call. I think more and more customers are going to openly challenge salespeople about the extent of their knowledge. Without the benefit of planning, you put yourself in a perilous situation, sitting in the customer's office with a look on your face that resembles a deer caught in the headlights. The show-off stage of PSIP is an excellent way to differentiate yourself, not to mention the confidence derived from having conversational knowledge about your potential customer.

Inform. The Inform stage of PSIP provides an opportunity to inform your customer about what you are selling and the reason for your visit. I refer to this stage as *synchronizing the call;* advising the customer of your call objectives. This helps align your call agenda to the customer's buying agenda. Amazingly, customers are often subjected to long-winded feature dumps, but are never really sure what the objective is or what the sales representative is trying to accomplish. I have witnessed calls where the customer and the salesperson are completely out of sync. The expectations of each are totally different. Perhaps I should have titled this book, *Synchronized Selling.*

Getting in sync with your customer means asking a few up-front questions to evaluate his or her understanding of what you represent. Ask, "Have you heard of our company before?" and "Do you know what we do?" If the customer answers no to either question, give a quick overview of who you are and what you are selling. Synchronize the call. Don't feature dump them with reams of useless information, but rather respond with an informative two- to three-minute information statement. Consider this your corporate *infomercial.* To add impact to your information statement, include a few key benefits that previous customers have come to appreciate. This stage of PSIP need not take more than three to five minutes. Brevity is a virtue.

Probe. The entrepreneurial style of selling places emphasis on probing for needs and expectations, exploring for an opportunity to satisfy an existing inconvenience or dissatisfaction with a current vendor. Skillful use of questions is the essence of an effective needs analysis, which of course is the prerequisite to a creative, tailored solution. Creative solutions drive the relationship. There is a direct correlation between the success of salespeople and their *confidence* to ask superior questions. The challenge is not the ability to ask questions but rather the confidence to ask enough of the right questions. I have seen countless situations where salespeople make the mistake of asking only a few scripted questions then launch into an enthusiastic, well-rehearsed feature dump based on what they think *should* be of interest to the customer. Rarely do they plan the questions they will ask. Sales entrepreneurs realize that the questions you ask customers are more important than anything you tell them. By answering questions, customers state their ideas, thoughts, and needs in their own words. If they say it, it's true. If you say it, they can doubt you. They quickly sense your presentation (feature dump) is based on your own self-serving interests, and the reaction is sure to be negative. You must be interested, as well as interesting. Imagine the impression you would create on a blind date if you did most of the talking and didn't ask any questions. It wouldn't make for a very interesting conversation. I don't think there would be a second date; just as there won't be a second appointment with a potential customer.

Most customers divulge as little as possible, especially during the early stage of the call. Unless you probe with smart questions, they give you only average information. Dumb questions begets dumb information, which means you deliver a dumb solution. Dumb information means it's the same information your competitor received. Your customer will tell you that your solution is dumb by saying, "Interesting, that's exactly what your competitor told me." Superior questions help you avoid the me-too presentation, the cookie-cutter syndrome. Customers purchase differences, not similarities. Don't be caught sitting in your customer's office giving new meaning to the movie *Dumb and Dumber.*

Unfortunately few salespeople exploit the tremendous benefits that superior questions have on the selling relationship. The effective use of superior questions moves the selling process forward at a steady but unpressured pace while achieving your call agenda of discovering precisely what your customer's needs are. Your objective is to lead your customer to a higher level of thinking. Your questions should stimulate the customer to go beyond conventional thinking and responses. Remember, the quality of your questions determines the quality of your solution. If you do not identify the customers' dominant buying motives—their hot-buttons—your solution will be no better, and no different than your competitors. Differentiate yourself by asking smart questions and avoid the risk of being perceived as a commodity, a me-too solution. Probe in a manner that communicates sincerity, genuine interest, and empathy. You and your customer are engaged in a dialogue, a fluid, seamless conversation exploring the possibility of a win-win relationship.

Probe Architecture: Peel the Onion

I use the word architecture because that's what needs to happen: You must design smart questions to ask. Probes unquestionably persuade more powerfully than any other form of verbal behavior. The success of a sales call depends more than anything else on how thorough your needs analysis is. The effort you invest in developing and asking smart questions to uncover customer needs, biases, perceptions, and fears that are not normally revealed to salespeople will pay off handsomely. The ultimate prize will go to the one who asks the best questions. I refer to the practice of asking smart questions as *peeling the onion*. As with dicing an onion, stupid questions (common questions) may cause your customer's eyes to glaze over and communicate impatience. The more layers you can peel away from suspicious, apprehensive customers, the sooner you get to the heart of their needs. Ask stupid questions and you get useless information, probably the same information your competitor walked away with. I think Werner Heisberg, a Nobel Prize-winning physicist, said it best, "Nature does not reveal its secrets, it only responds to our method of questioning."

The object is to design probes to encourage your customers to reveal their needs—peel the onion. Standard practice is to distinguish between open and closed probes, but don't limit yourself to only these two.

Open probes are used to get the customer talking, to divulge information, and to perhaps reveal unexpected information. They get the prospect to explain and talk openly about their business and current situation. Open probes generate a talkative, conversational response. Some authors suggest the five Ws (who, what, where, when, or why) are good open questions to start with. I disagree. I consider them closed questions that can often be answered with one- or two-word answers. I offer the following open probe prompts:

- Tell me about . . .
- Explain to me . . .
- In what way . . .
- Help me understand . . .
- Can you elaborate . . .
- Share with me . . .
- Please tell me how . . .
- How else . . .
- What do you mean by . . .

- What are your thoughts/ideas/experiences/reflections . . .

- If you could build or design the perfect _____, what would it look like . . . ?

These are excellent, field-tested prompts used to encourage a talkative response. Simply tell your customer up front that you need to ask questions to better understand their business. Customers love to talk about their business, their job, and their company. You can't ask too many questions. However, if your customer becomes impatient with your questioning, simply restate your objective and perhaps reschedule another appointment. Don't let their anxiousness draw you into a response before you understand their business. Be patient.

Closed probes are used to get very specific information. They usually limit the response to one-word answers. Closed probes are less powerful and have an uncanny ability to increase tension. They can be intimidating to certain personality styles. The other concern is that they end the conversation. Once a closed probe is answered you have to start another conversation. Closed probes should only be used for verification, commitment, or confirming (closing). Examples of closed prompts include the words:

• do	• won't
• have	• can
• are	• can't
• will	• shall

An excellent strategy to help identify the decision maker (the bag of money) is to use these three closed probes when talking with your customer or with senior management:

1. Do you (Does X) make the decisions?

2. Do you (Does X) have a budget?

3. Do you (Does X) talk with anyone else prior to a decision?

My experience shows that the customer will answer yes to the first two questions but introduce a second party when asked the third question. This is a red flag because the additional person is often the final decision maker. You must understand who is involved and how the final decision is made. Your objective now is to get an audience with that person, hopefully with the support of your initial contact. This simple strategy is so overlooked and yet effective that it alone will help increase your close ratio. We often waste a lot of time by getting sucked into dealing with the wrong people, people who think they have the final authority to purchase.

Reflective probes are used to identify personal biases of the customer, which is exactly what you want. Customers often answer questions with an eye to the corporation, answering with the best interests of the corporation in mind. However, you need to differentiate yourself by understanding and satisfying the personal biases and preferences of the buyer, the bag of money. Reflective probes are very effective for drawing out background information, personal feelings, and opinions. To get past common corporate responses, ask uncommon questions. Design specific, reflective probes, that encourage your customer to tell you things not told to the competition. The decision to buy from you will be based on satisfying both corporate needs as well as personal biases and preferences. Your customer can decide on vendor A or B, both are capable of doing a good job, but the final decision comes down to which vendor recognized and satisfied all aspects of their decision. For example, the customer may only have two years' experience with the current company but 15 years' experience in the industry. You want to tap into his or her total experience. That information can help you design a solution that satisfies both corporate needs and personal biases. In the training business, role playing is a good example—some customers like them and some are biased against feeling they are too artificial and ineffective. Know the human side of your customer. The key is to recognize your customer's work experience and ask well-designed reflective probes. Reflective probes include the words:

- feel
- opinion
- perception
- sense
- personally

- aware
- belief
- view
- experience
- previous

Examples include; "What are your personal feelings about . . .?" or "What is your perception of . . .?" or "What is your previous experience with . . .?" A favorite of mine is "If it were" your company what would you do?" That usually gets them going.

You'll be amazed at the unexpected responses, yet pleased with the helpful information reflective probes reveal.

Conversational probes represent a style of questioning that is gaining in popularity. I have been experimenting with conversational probes, and along with other sales entrepreneurs I have found that it's a much more relaxed, natural approach. Conversational probes are used to start, encourage, and maintain a *normal* conversation. The questions themselves are not anything special or unique, but I suggest it's a matter of using a mixture of open, closed, and reflective probes while pursing a normal conversation.

Quite frankly, I suggest you quit worrying about labeling your probes opened or closed and simply ask your customer a series of smart questions and enjoy a professional, social type of conversation. Continue your conversational probes until all the customer's needs and expectations have been explored and all the parameters to a possible solution have been covered. In other words, keep asking questions until a solution presents itself, until a 100-watt light bulb goes off in your head with a solution that excites both you and your customer. I would suggest that in a typical sales call you should be asking upwards of 50–60 questions. A lot of these questions are what I refer to as clarification questions. For example, if the customer responds to your "What is important to you?" question with "Service is important" then you must clarify it by asking "What does good service look like to you?" Likewise, if they respond with "Quality is important" or "Delivery is important" you must clarify by asking exactly what they mean by quality or delivery. The danger is sales representatives are far too zealous to respond rather than taking the time to fully understand the customers' issues. Hence, by using a combination of conversational, reflective, and clarification probes, it doesn't take long to ask 50–60 questions.

Should our communication strategy change when talking to a customer versus a friend or spouse? It shouldn't. Keep it simple and relaxed. I've yet to hear a salesperson say, "I look forward to getting home and asking my spouse a bunch of open and closed probes!" Imagine your spouse responding with, "Honey, I'd appreciate it if you didn't ask me so many closed probes, please ask me more open probes." Sounds a little ridiculous, I agree. My point is this: Why be guided by a mechanical, clinical approach to probing during the day, then take a relaxed, more natural social approach with friends and family. Adapt one simple, consistent approach that accommodates both business and social interactions. You will feel a lot more confident and relaxed in both kinds of interactions.

How often has your sales manager questioned you about open or closed probes? I've yet to hear a sales manager ask, "Sounds like you had a great call. Congratulations. Tell me, how many open and closed probes did you ask?" Who cares! As if we don't have enough to think about during a sales call. The point is you closed the sale with a win-win solution.

I appreciate that my probing approach may be unconventional, but it's proving to be a simple, less stressful approach and is certainly appreciated by my customers. It's a refreshing change for both parties.

In their unbridled enthusiasm or nervousness, salespeople often overlook an important aspect of the discovery stage— asking permission to ask questions. Asking permission can be as simple as, "Ms. Smith, we've been able to help hundreds of companies with various training solutions. We may be able to help you. I don't know if we can or not but to determine that, may I ask you a few questions?" Alternatively, you might ask, "To make the best use of our time today I'd like to ask you a few questions. Would you mind?" By asking permission, you help relax the situation. Your customer becomes a willing participant in the task of finding a possible solution that makes life a little easier.

Once you have their permission (which will be 99.9% of the time), you now have license to proceed with a series of planned, well-thought-out questions. The secrets to a smooth and speedy close are often contained in the answers. Your customer's answers help pinpoint the area where you may be able to help them. It's like a game. Questions unlock the secrets to closing the sale; ask the right questions, get the right information, and present the right solution. The quality of your questions and your confidence to ask them in a logical, fluid sequence is what demonstrates to the potential customer that you are a competent professional.

Tim Commandment #5

Use quality questions to unlock the secrets to confirming more sales.
Ask: Am I asking enough smart questions?
Do I understand their needs and expectations?

As the questioning proceeds, your customer is drawn more and more into the conversation because answering demands total attention. The average person speaks at approximately 130 words per minute, but can think at approximately 1,000 words per minute. While you are talking (feature dumping) it's very easy for the customer to listen as well as think about other things including possible objections, problems at work or home, an argument with the teenager last night, missing a Visa payment, or the prediction of rain for tomorrow's 2:30 tee-off time. Questions minimize *mental drift* and help keep control of the sales call. The longer you talk, the more opportunity the customer has to *drift* into another world. However, the instant you ask a question the customer snaps back to the conversation and refocuses on you. Control lies with the person asking the questions. Your goal is to do more listening than talking. As long as you're talking, you're going to hear stuff you already know. Think about it. To learn, you must be silent and listen. By the way, silent and listen contain the same letters and I find it interesting that *ear* is found in *learn* and *earn*.

Your needs analysis will reveal one of three possible scenarios. The customer is aware of your product but is currently using the competition and is not interested in you; the customer is unfamiliar with your product and shows no interest; or the customer is unaware of your product but expresses an interest. The latter is what I call creating demand—introducing a product or service never used before by an existing or a potential customer. Demand is created by understanding the customers' needs and presenting the product or service as a benefit to their business. Customers are always on the lookout for a competitive edge. The introduction of your product or service

It seems all I do is answer questions. It's exhausting. Maybe I should be the one asking the questions.

just might help to achieve that competitive edge. However, you must appreciate that even though you created the initial demand, the customer may invite your competition to present their product for comparative reasons and to validate the legitimacy of the new product or service.

Of the three possible scenarios, the first one is most common: A customer has a need but is currently using a competitor. Thus, your goal is to ask carefully planned questions that encourage the customer to review the performance of an existing supplier. Your questions may reveal some instances of poor service or quality. Through this tactful method you do not criticize your competitor; your customer does.

Some authors suggest that selling is a "hurt and rescue" business. Find the hurt, uncover the pain, discover the problem, and come to the rescue. This concept suggests that the customer has been living with an intolerable situation and that your product or service will provide instant relief from all suffering. Sales representatives buy into this concept thinking customers are suffering from a gaping wound that only their product or service will heal. Wrong! The reality is that your potential customer is doing just fine without you or your remedy for instant relief. The challenge is to discover an inconvenience or dissatisfaction that the customer is experiencing with their existing vendor, and then provide a solution that resolves it. Even though the customer is somewhat satisfied, your solution must focus on alleviating the inconvenience. Otherwise, why would they switch to you? They won't.

An inconvenience is a situation that is less than ideal, but your customer is prepared to tolerate it. The customer may feel that fixing it may not be worth the effort, or a different vendor might make things worse. I suggest that it may only be an inconvenience because as I mentioned earlier, your competition mirrors approximately 90% or more of your features so you know they are doing a pretty good job servicing the customer. Very few products or services are perceived as providing a unique advantage.

Differences between competitors are much more subtle today than perhaps even five years ago. Today we sell in an intensely competitive marketplace. Enhanced competition, pressures to differentiate and global impact have made even the best features and benefits temporary as well as tenuous. Often the customer is left struggling to sort out the differences. Remember, your customers buy from you based on less than 5% of your features. Unfortunately, price becomes the easiest and quickest way for a customer to validate differences between competitors and justify a purchase. That's why price gets the attention it does.

By asking a series of smart, well-thought-out questions, customers will reveal clues as to the features that will satisfy the sale. Just as in baking or cooking, there must be the right mix of ingredients (features) to produce the desired results.

Feature Fishing

Now it's time to go fishing. Just hang on, I don't mean taking the day off to head out to your favorite fishing hole. I'm referring to fishing right in the customer's office, *verbal casting.* Bait the conversation with questions that reveal the customer's needs, expectations, and hot-buttons. Although you have done your pre-call planning on the macro issues, you cannot learn intimate knowledge of your customer's business until you engage in a conversation. During this conversation your objective is to fish around to discover the features on your menu that may be of interest.

I offer two methods of feature fishing: 1) Simply ask your customer what's important when considering a supplier. What specifics is he or she looking for? What are his or her expectations? What makes a good vendor? 2) Suggest some of your more popular features by scrolling through your menu. Ask the customer: "Have you thought about . . . ?" "Have you considered . . . ?" "Did you know that . . . ?" "Have you ever used . . . ?" and so on. It's the same as your server in a restaurant recommending daily specials. The answers to your probes help identify specific requirements, information you wouldn't glean from an annual report or the receptionist. Personally, I prefer a combination of the two methods.

Effective Bridging

Once you have identified the appropriate features and the hot-buttons, it's time to bridge. *Bridging* occurs when you link the feature to the benefit. Each feature offers several potential benefits that must be explained in detail for the customer to fully appreciate it as a benefit. In the end, the customer decides if the feature is in fact a benefit. Remember, customers buy benefits, not features. Features on their own represent the so-what information I spoke of earlier. Don't feature dump.

Although this book is not about scripts and rigid steps to follow, I do suggest you consider this very short, succinct script while you get comfortable with bridging, "The benefit to you is . . . " These five words verbally initiate the bridge, taking a feature to a benefit. Once the feature is bridged to a benefit, confirm its acceptance by asking, "Do you see this (feature) as a benefit to you and your business?" If your customer agrees, you have successfully bridged the feature and anchored it as a benefit. The following diagram illustrates bridging.

BRIDGING

Features	Potential Benefits
1. _____	_____
2. _____	_____
3. _____	_____
4. _____	_____
5. _____	_____
6. _____	_____
7. _____	_____

The above illustration represents the three steps of effective bridging.

Step 1:   In conversation with your customer, features #2, #5
           and #7 were identified as hot-buttons, relevant fea-
           tures. The other features proved to be of little inter-
           est, so-what information. Continue to verbally scroll
           your menu until you have identified three or four
           features of interest.

Step 2:   Bridge appropriate features using the statement,
           "The benefit to you is . . . " This statement ensures
           your customer is thinking in terms of benefits. Go
           on to explain the benefits of the feature in terms of
           your customer's specific requirements and how the
           benefits relate to his or her needs.

Step 3:   Validate the customer's acceptance of the benefits by
           asking, "Do you see this (feature) as a benefit?" If
           yes, you have benefits.

Bridging is a fundamental ingredient of a successful call.
When followed, the three steps eliminate the monotony of feature dumping, identify a tailored solution, shorten the sales cycle
and show customers how you can help their business. Benefits
sell, features tell.

Inverse Bridging

Inverse bridging occurs when you start with a benefit and
bridge it back to the supporting feature. This approach says to
the customer, "This is what we can do for you (benefit) and this
is how we do it (feature)." This is an excellent strategy to make
a telephone appointment, to create demand in a new or existing account, or to gain interest when making cold calls.
Customers frequently challenge salespeople by demanding,
"Why should I see you?" or "How can you help my business?"
or "I'm too busy, call me in three months." Sound familiar?
When on the telephone the challenge is to get the customer's

attention quickly and sell the appointment. Features rarely get attention quickly, but by stating a benefit right up front you may bait the prospect enough to stimulate mild curiosity. The question is, what benefits do you use to stimulate interest? My advice is to use the benefits that have proven popular with current customers. Do some research. Know the benefits of your product or service that are consistently accepted by your customer base. Alternatively, offer a benefit that you know will directly impact your customer's business. Remember, it is the customer who validates your benefit so don't be shocked if they reject your initial attempt at inverse bridging. If they do, simply acknowledge their indifference and suggest other benefits that may be more relevant. The objective with inverse bridging is not to sell them, but to gain access. The following illustration shows inverse bridging.

INVERSE BRIDGING

Features   Potential Benefits

1. _____   _____

2. _____   _____

3. _____   _____

4. _____   _____

5. _____   _____

6. _____   _____

7. _____   _____

Every salesperson at some point in time has experienced the frustration of trying to make appointments. One approach that has proven effective is to suggest to the potential customer during the initial telephone conversation that you may not have anything to sell him or her. If they ask, "What are you going to sell me?" simply respond with, "At this point, I'm not sure—maybe nothing. However, what I would like is 15 minutes of your time to explore the possibility of our companies doing business." The very suggestion that you are not trying to sell them something will get the customer's attention. They will feel more relaxed about granting you an appointment. The use of inverse bridging and the "maybe nothing" statement is a potent combination that will increase your success with first-time appointments. Participants at my seminars agree that this approach is unconventional but they recognize how it can be immensely effective.

Avoid the Penalty Box

The penalty box is a very crowded, impoverished place where sales representatives frequently find themselves. However, a visit to the penalty box can easily go undetected. The problem is twofold: Sales representatives not only don't realize they're there; or worse, they don't know why they were sent there.

A visit to the penalty box occurs when the salesperson has relinquished control of the sales call by immediately answering the customer's question. Salespeople tend to answer questions too quickly, failing to determine why the question was asked in the first place. Have you ever stopped to wonder why a customer is asking you a question? If you remove *your* assumptions, the answer is, "I don't know why he asked that." You run the danger of committing to an answer *prior* to understanding the customer's reason for asking it. Eagerly answering all his questions immediately can have dire consequences to the outcome of a sales call.

You can maintain control of the sales call by answering high-impact questions *with* a question. Customers usually have a good reason for asking a question, so it's in your best interest to find out why. What might be in the back of their minds? What's the motivation behind the question? Jumping on the question with a quick, clever answer simply gives up control. You are totally at the mercy of the customer's interpretation of your answer. A visit to the penalty box is one of the biggest reasons salespeople lose sales.

The problem stems from the process we were taught in our educational system. We were conditioned by our teachers and parents to, "Just answer the question." In class we were taught to raise our hand and spit out an answer. When answered correctly, it fueled self-esteem and heightened our confidence, especially in the presence of our classmates and our teachers. Sales entrepreneurs have learned to resist the temptation to immediately respond to questions, but rather to inquire about the reason for asking. I offer this five-step strategy to help you safeguard yourself against unproductive time spent in the penalty box.

1. Identify the question as either high impact or low impact. Ask, "What impact will my answer have on the buying decision?" A high-impact question means your answer will either negatively or positively impact the customer's decision to buy from you. You must listen carefully to the question, put it in the context of the conversation, and decide on your answer's impact. If high impact, go to Step 2. If low impact, simply answer the question.

2. Compliment their question—make them feel good. Thank them for asking you a good question, one that perhaps you haven't heard before. It may have been asked because of its importance or relevancy to the situation but you won't know until you ask. In any case, be sure to acknowledge the question as a good one.

3. Identify the agenda. Why is the customer asking the question? At this point, only the customer knows. Politely probe the reason for asking. You need to be delicate with this because you don't want to appear confrontational by blurting out, "Why do you ask?" Your response should sound like this: "That's a good question, I've never been asked that before. Would you share with me your reason for asking?" Articulate your response to the question using your own words, your own style. The customer will usually share some thoughts, helping you pinpoint exact concerns.

Echoing can also be an effective method to reveal your customer's hidden agenda. When the customer finishes asking a question, simply repeat or echo a couple of key words from the question. For example, a customer says, "Your delivery schedule seems to be too long!" Your respond with, "Too long?" Your echo will stimulate a response.

4. Bridge. Now that you understand the customer's reason for asking, bridge the appropriate feature to the benefit. For example, if he were curious or uncertain about delivery and Step 3 revealed that he wants rush deliveries when required, you can scroll your features menu and pick one that best satisfies that particular need, then bridge it as a benefit.

5. Verify. Ask the customer, "Have I answered your question? Have I addressed your concern?" Do not press forward with the sales call until you have satisfied his concern. Earning the right to advance means leaving behind no unresolved questions, concerns, or objections.

To illustrate the five steps, let's look at a fairly typical scenario. A relatively new salesperson is calling on a potential A account who is doing business with the salesperson's biggest competitor. Midway through the sales call, the customer asks:

C: How long have you been in the industry? (high-impact question)

S: That's a good question that I'm often asked and I'll be happy to answer it. Is experience something you are looking for in a salesperson?

C: Yes it is. I want someone with no fewer than 10 to 12 years of industry experience. Our business is unique and we rely on our suppliers to keep us current with industry trends and new technologies.

S: Although I've only been in the business for two years, I have a wealth of knowledge and support at the office. In fact our group represents over 100 man-years of experience. The benefit to you is that as your salesperson, I can put that experience to work for you.

C: True enough. I didn't consider things from that angle.

S: Have I addressed your concern?

C: Yes, that makes sense.

You have now earned the right to continue. The response was both honest *and* right. These five steps should only serve as a guideline to managing the sales dialogue. The concept of answering a question with a question is not new, it's been around for decades. However, I am simply packaging the process in a professional, manageable format. The objective is to foster appreciation and respect for your customer's question; take a moment to pause, and consider why it is being asked. Even when you provide an honest answer, it may not be the right one. Of course all of your answers will be honest, but are they the *best* answers? There is a big difference. Our answers must align themselves with the customer's agenda. I'm not suggesting that avoiding the penalty box is a new sales gimmick or a manipulative maneuver, it's not. It's simply an effective tactic to *synchronize* the call. Now take a moment and imagine the consequences of just blurting out an honest answer.

C: How long have you been in the industry?

S: Two years. I started just after we moved into our new building.

C: Really.

S: Yeah, so let me just finish up what I was talking to you about.

Although the answer of "two years" is honest, it was the wrong one. The customer now tells you, "Well, thanks for coming by. I've got your brochures and pricing, we'll keep you on file." You just got sent to the penalty box, and chances are you have no idea why. Customers interpret your answers based on their biases and perceptions. In this case, the customer hears the answer "two years" and interprets that as having no experience. It was honest, but wrong. Honesty and right must work together, you can't have one without the other; otherwise you're in the penalty box. If nothing else, this concept will heighten your awareness of how important it is to pay attention to customers' questions and avoid the penalty box.

Communication Skills

Effective communication is essential for a successful sale but is probably one of the most overlooked, underdeveloped skills in professional selling. We cannot take communication for granted simply because we are fluent in the English language—but we do. The cornerstone of effective communication is sensitivity to the needs of others. It begins with an understanding of the communication process. *Encoding* occurs when a sender translates thoughts into a message. The receiver must *decode* the message and try to understand what the sender intended to communicate. Communication is effective only when the receiver accurately understands what the sender intended to transmit. It's not uncommon to hear someone say, "Yeah, but that's not what I meant" or "I thought you said this . . . "

Communication in selling involves more than presenting your product or service; it involves an active, two-way exchange of ideas and thoughts. However, research suggests that in most calls salespeople do up to 60% of the talking.[1] Wrong thing to do. Remember PEZ, Please Excuse my Zealousness. We often think of ourselves as good communicators because we have the gift of the gab. I know of several people who were encouraged to pursue a career in sales because they were great talkers. We equate speaking with control and power, assuming the spotlight is focused on the talkers rather than the listeners. Our society recognizes and rewards great orators, actors, singers, public speakers, and news commentators who excel at one-way communication. There are lots of books and seminars on developing public speaking skills but when did you ever hear of a seminar on public listening skills? They don't exist. Unfortunately, listening is not the sexy part of the communication model. I would suggest that the biggest violation of the communication model is poor listening skills.

Why We Are Poor Listeners

Lazy listening is enormously costly to our success. Most of us *think* we are good listeners, but that overconfidence may be the reason for our downfall. Nothing puts a sales call in jeopardy faster than poor, inattentive listening. Customers don't take long to get a sense of your listening commitment, especially given the fact that 90% of communication is nonverbal.[2] That's right, 90%. About 55% is through obvious body language and 35% is by how you say it.[2] Given these overwhelming statistics, it's pretty tough to convince the customer that you are listening if in fact you're not.

We listen at about 25% of our potential. We miss, ignore, forget, distort, or misunderstand 75% of what we hear.[3] Hard to believe perhaps, but true. Given these statistics, we can see why communication breaks down so quickly. The receiver is responding to only 25% of the sender's message.[3] That's why during my seminars I suggest that, "In most cases, communication is not part of the conversation." Such lazy listening habits are very costly, to both your business and your personal success.

Improvement begins with an understanding of why people have a natural tendency to be poor listeners. Rather than have you put this book down and promise aloud, "I will be a better listener," I offer you the four reasons why we are poor listeners.

1. Our predominant thoughts focus on *ourselves* and *sex*. We think of ourselves 24 hours a day—how we look, feel, our personal problems and successes, work, and so on. Even while we sleep. Did you ever have a dream where you weren't in it? Probably not. We see ourselves as the most important element of our lives, followed by a natural attraction to sex. Psychologists agree that on average we think of sex consciously or unconsciously every two and a half minutes. We were put on this planet to reproduce, so thank goodness He made it fun. Maslow's hierarchy of needs theory reinforces this concept, along with our overwhelming need to be loved and accepted. People will go to great lengths to satisfy those needs. It's no wonder we are poor listeners when sitting with our customers. Our agendas usually take precedence over theirs.

2. Our minds wander. Our minds think approximately eight times faster than we talk. We normally *speak* at approximately 130 words per minute, we *listen* and understand at up to 400 words per minute, and we can *think* at 1,000 words per minute. Unbelievable but true. Here's the dilemma: our customers talk to us at 130 words per minute and we think at 1,000 words per minute. Mental drift is too easy and often results in minimal communication during a conversation. Clearly, it takes tremendous discipline to stay focused on the customer's message. By the way, your customers also experience mental drift at a speed of 1,000 words per minute. Chances are good that during a feature dump their minds will wander off somewhere else, perhaps Jamaica or Barbados.

3. We can't wait to reply. Our unbridled enthusiasm to reply sabotages the communication model. We often listen with the sole intent to reply. At the expense of effective listening we formulate a response, at a speed of 1,000 words per minute, before the sender has completed commenting. The second they finish speaking we jump in with what we think is a valid, appropriate response. Our quick response is further fueled by our perceptions and biases as we attempt to decode their message. When you jump in with your quick response, it clearly communicates to the sender that you were not listening, that you were more concerned with your reply rather than understanding the message. It can be very frustrating and irritating when you know the listener is not paying attention and is preoccupied with formulating a response.

Listening is a lot easier when you like the person and agree with the message. The most difficult time to listen is when you disagree with what you're seeing or hearing. Under those conditions, many listeners aren't listening at all—they're preoccupied with drafting a rebuttal. The challenge is to put personal

feelings aside and focus on the message. As with effective negotiation, deal with the issues, not the personalities.

A suggestion to help overcome your tendency to offer an
immediate reply is to wait two to three seconds before you reply.
Let the sender finish her comments, look her in the eye,
acknowledge her input with a nod or a verbal sign, then reply.
The big plus is that if you wait a moment your customer may
start talking again and yes, that's a good thing.

4. **We interrupt—a lot.** Everybody has an opinion and
loves to get his two cents' worth in. Even if we aren't asked, we
willingly lend our views and comments, thinking that we are
making a significant contribution. Over the years we have been
conditioned to interrupt, or we may not get a chance to share
our views, which of course are critical if the conversation is
going to have any substance. What fuels our need to interrupt is
that we are always thinking of self or sex and we can do it at
1,000 words per minute. With this lethal combination it's no
wonder we are poor listeners.

Effective listening means more than refraining from the bad
habit of interrupting. Good listening means being satisfied to
listen to the entire message rather than waiting impatiently to
jump in with your response.

My informal research suggests that a conversation won't last
longer than 20 to 30 seconds before an interruption occurs—
someone jumping in with a story, another view. However, in a
sales call it can be advantageous to interrupt with questions that
clarify your understanding of the situation. I refer to this as *productive interruption*. Customers are tolerant of clarification questions because the focus remains on them and you are showing
interest.

To further demonstrate your commitment to the customer and to improve your listening skills, be sure to take notes during the sales call. There is no way you will remember all the details and issues you discussed. In regard to note-taking protocol, be sure to ask permission to take notes when you are in the customer's office. It's polite, respectful, and your nonverbal message is, "This meeting is important so I need to take some notes." If you are in the neutral territory of a boardroom or a meeting room, you do not need permission. However, ask anyway. If the customer is getting ahead of you and your note-taking, simply interrupt the customer by saying, "That's a great point, let me make a note of that." The customer will be happy to give you a few seconds to complete your notes. At the end of the meeting you might consider summarizing the important points. You can preface this with, "As I understand it . . ."

When you improve your listening skills, you hold a competitive edge. Lucky for you, listening gets scant recognition by your competitors. As we know, listening is not strongly identified in selling and you are not likely to be "out-listened" by the competition. They're too busy trying to get the customer to listen.

NOTES

1. Customer Based Research Conducted by Spectrum Training Solutions Inc.

2. Dugger, Jim. *Learn to Listen*. Page 14. 1992. National Press Publications.

3. Bone, Diane. *The Business of Listening: A Practical Guide to Effective Listening*. Page 5, 1988. Crisp Publications Inc.

Congratulations, you have now completed
Step #5

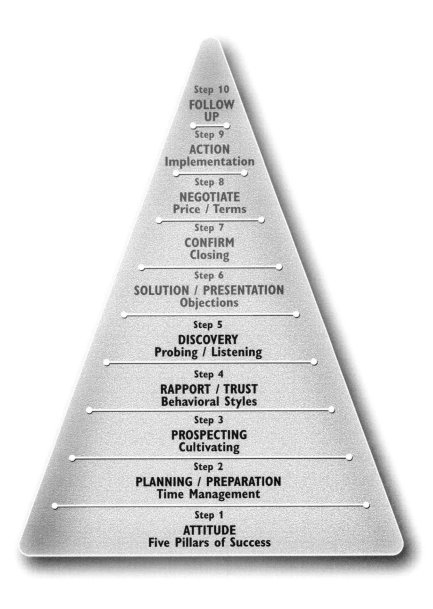

Chapter 8

PRESENTATION SKILLS: VALUE-ADDED SOLUTIONS

Congratulations on another graduation. You have successfully worked through the first five steps of the Sequential Model, doing the groundwork to meet and exceed your customers' expectations. This next step applies to potential new customers as well as existing customers to whom you are presenting a new product or service.

So what is a value-added solution? It means enhancing your solution by *exceeding* the expectations of your customers. It means going outside the traditional role of a sales representative to provide a solution that truly elevates you above your closest competitor. Customers buy differences, not similarities. The challenge is finding innovative, unique ways to exceed expectations. Cookie-cutter solutions and boring, ho-hum presentations are all too common. As Larry Wilson writes in his book, *Changing the Game:* "Instead of trying to find prospects who fit my presentation, what I needed to do was fit my presentation to the prospect I found.[1] A simple idea, but it changed selling for me." Unfortunately for customers, sales representatives continue to try to fit them into canned, rehearsed presentations. Or they try to close the sale based on price, instead of offering a value-added solution. Sadly enough, customers are often saddled with the burden of trying to differentiate among proposals that imitate each other—me-too, cookie-cutter solutions that seduce customers with little more than the lowest price. Your responsibility is to make it easy for your customer to decide, to remove the stress of uncertainty.

Why Should I Buy From You?

"Why should I buy from you?" is a universal question, one that "stalls the call" and puts salespeople into a tailspin, struggling with a response that does little to excite the customer. I've seen it happen far too often. Openly challenged, the salesperson retreats deep into his or her comfort zone responding with a well-rehearsed feature dump, hoping to avoid a crash and burn situation. We know the result all too well. Another presentation ending in tragedy, another lost sale.

The "Why should I buy from you?" question needs to be answered with a well-prepared presentation that addresses the benefits of both parties doing business together. Your success relies on how well you probed, identified expectations, and then satisfied those expectations by presenting the attributes your company can offer. Don't make the all-too-common mistake of telling your story from your point of view, but rather present your story from the customers' point of view. You must weave appropriate benefits into your presentation so that customers clearly see your solution as helping their business run more efficiently. True story: Two gentlemen were getting their hair cut. Person A was a VP at a large oil company and person B was the president of a different company. Person A knew B and introduced himself and his company saying, "My people were recently in to see your people." Person B responded by saying, in his Texas accent, "That's interesting. What you-all goin' to do for us?" I couldn't have said it any better myself. Customers expect innovative, value-added solutions that become assets to their business. If you are doing a good job, you should be aware of your customers' expectations. Your presentation does not happen in isolation. It is supported by the first five steps of the Sequential Model, including a thorough Discovery step, earning the right to present. Remember, your model allows for no missing pieces.

Neutralize the Competition

Creative sellers get the sale and the gold medal. Through effective Discovery, sales entrepreneurs work with customers to present creative solutions that exceed expectations. *Exceeding* is the key, the essence of a convincing presentation. If you simply *meet* their expectations, that's just doing your job, no big deal, so what? Sales entrepreneurs ask themselves; "How can I use my imagination and creativity to make a vivid impression on my customer? How can I make my presentation different and stronger?" Eliminate routine, boring, *predictable* presentations." Chances are your customer has endured hundreds of me-too presentations, so make yours different, make it fun. The key to neutralizing your competition is innovation.

Ten Key Ingredients

To help you differentiate yourself and neutralize the competition, I offer ten key ingredients of an effective, creative presentation. They apply whether you are presenting to an individual, a committee, or a group.

1. Enjoy Yourself. Enjoy what you are doing. Selling is fun, not a battle of wits between customer and salesperson, so loosen up and enjoy. Believe in yourself and what you are selling, supported by the right mental attitude. Add your own style of enthusiasm and be somewhat entertaining as well as informative.

After all, you are on stage. Communicate your belief in yourself and your product or service by exhibiting sincere enthusiasm. Involve your customer when and if appropriate. I tell my customers that I sell enter*train*ment. At my seminars you're going to learn something but you will have fun in the process. When was the last time you learned something that was boring or presented in lackluster fashion? You probably haven't—boredom stifles learning. Rekindle your enthusiasm if necessary and present with gusto.

Another aspect of enjoying yourself is looking good, feeling good. I often suggest the most important presentation of the day is to yourself in the mirror. You must be confident of your appearance prior to a confident delivery. People love to visualize and the *visual* sense is very, very powerful. In fact, it is the visual impression that makes the greatest impact. Remember, people buy you with their eyes within 10 seconds. As a result, our verbal content can be virtually smothered by the vocal and visual components.

Research suggests that the believability of a message is evaluated on three elements; 7 percent verbal, 38 percent vocal, and 55 percent visual.[2] "What you do speaks so loud I can't hear what you say." Great words spoken by Ralph Emerson.

The fun of it all begins with the process of looking and feeling good. Don your best outfit, fill your lungs with confidence, and within ten seconds your audience will be impressed with your presentation.

2. Prepare and prepare some more. Preparation is key to a smooth, fluid presentation. Any good seminar on presentation skills will tell you, "Don't try to eliminate the butterflies, simply get them to fly in formation." Having the butterflies is a form of positive energy that will help you get started and make a smooth transition into the body of your presentation. Here is a guideline that I use: Every five minutes of presentation time requires one hour of preparation time. Thus, a 15-minute presentation requires a minimum of three hours preparation. Trust me, this formula works. As one anonymous quote suggests, "Every time you open your mouth, your mind is on parade." Preparation will ensure your parade looks sharp, sounds sharp, and dazzles your audience. Make it fresh, not canned.

Another suggestion is to rehearse your presentation by delivering it aloud to a wall. Pick a quiet place, perhaps at home, stand back from a wall then go through your presentation, at least the verbal part. If you do it a couple of times to the wall, you'll be amazed how easy it is when you do it live.

As a professional keynote speaker, I spend days preparing for a half-day keynote. Here is another guideline: Be cognizant of *when* you prepare. Don't use valuable selling hours to do your homework. I refer you back to Tim Commandment #4 in Chapter 4 (page 97).

3. Know your customer's style type. Consider how you might design your presentation to appeal to different style types. A presentation to a Director should be totally different than to a Socializer or a Thinker. Each style has different expectations that cannot be ignored (Chapter 6).

Socializer. Must be fun, entertaining, and stimulating. Sell sizzle more than steak. Make your presentation colorful and upbeat, showing how your product or service will enhance your customer's status and visibility.

Director. Must be short, to the point, businesslike, outlining the main points. Time will be limited so don't waste it with unnecessary conversation or detail. Present the facts and the results they can expect to see. Give them options where they can make decisions.

Thinker. Must be logical, informative, and detail-oriented. Thinkers are very analytical, looking for accurate information, honesty, and reliability. Back up your presentation with supportive documentation and data and a lot of technological punch. Don't expect a decision that day. Thinkers need time to mull it over, working out any possible bugs. Arrange a specific time to follow up.

Relater. Must be sensitive to the people side of the business. Ask for opinions and feelings and show how your solution will be compatible with other departments within the company. Use lots of references and testimonials. Relaters need to know that other customers support your product or service. They tend to follow the norm, guided by routine, so don't make your solution too bizarre or outlandish.

When presenting to a committee or to more than one individual, tailor your presentation to the style type of the decision maker among the group. Identify who the key individual is prior to the meeting, and design your presentation and your approach to reflect his or her style. You cannot be all things to all people, so don't even try. It makes for a very awkward presentation if you try to satisfy everyone by floating among the four styles. I caution you. Don't present until you have determined who will be there and why. Don't ever go into a presentation blind; do your homework. If you can't meet committee members prior to the presentation, at least talk to them on the phone to determine their style and their role in the decision-making process.

4. Involve the senses. A Chinese proverb says: "Tell me, I'll forget. Show me, I may remember. Involve me, I'll understand." Up to 82% of what we learn is through sight. Take advantage of these findings and include visuals where you can, within reason. The more senses you can engage in your presentation, the better—visual, auditory, or kinesthetic (touch it, feel it). Research demonstrates that *visual* input makes the greatest impact. Psychologists agree that viewing something three times has a lasting impression and improves retention and recall. However, don't show up to your next presentation with 56 overheads colorfully presented on PowerPoint.

5. Be benefit-oriented. People don't buy what something is, they buy what something does. Avoid presenting your features, they do nothing to stimulate the customer into action. Benefits will. By talking about benefits you keep your customer's attention focused on the "what's in it for me" aspect. A sobering thought to consider when presenting: Your average customers will immediately forget 50% of what you told them and after only 48 hours will forget up to 75% of your message. Ouch! All the more reason to captivate your customers' attention by using all their senses, presenting benefits, and having fun.

6. Avoid corporate jargon. Nothing loses customers faster than confusion. Don't use gobbledegook that may confuse them; use their language and their lingo and provide explanations where appropriate. My suggestion is to present simple concepts first, then complex ones later in the presentation. Presenting simple concepts early will help warm the audience to your style and make it easier for them to understand the complex ones later. Customers are sceptical of razzle-dazzle presentations; straightforwardness and honesty should be your guideposts.

7. Exceed expectations. The first step is to know what 100% is, then exceed it. Know what your customer expects from you. You only learn that by asking. Unless you clearly understand what the 100% mark is, you run the risk of delivering a solution that falls short of expectations. Delivering a solution that you are excited about does little to advance the sale if it is only at 90% of customers' expectations. Once again, that may be the reason you get beat up on price. A 90% solution doesn't cut it, not nowadays.

To exceed expectations, you only have to go an extra inch, not an extra mile. All it takes is a little extra effort, giving customers something they didn't expect. Exceed expectations by delivering an extra unexpected 1%: The 1% solution. It really doesn't take much to exceed expectations. Just as little things can turn a customer off, little things will turn a customer on. An example of a 1% solution would be just as you are leaving the store with your new CD player, the salesperson you dealt with stops you at the door and says, "Thank you for your business, I appreciate it. Why don't you go over to the rack and pick out a free CD of your choice? It's on me." Would that impress you? No doubt it would. The potential return on positive word of mouth is certainly worth the investment of giving away a free CD. Keep in mind, though, no two customers are alike. Not every customer will appreciate a free CD so you will need to vary your 1% solutions. Each customer comes with a unique set of expectations and perceptions that must be revealed during the Discovery step. It stands to reason, then, that no two presentations or solutions will be the same. I suggest that from now on you deliver a solution that is 101% of expectations—underpromise and overdeliver. Don't simply satisfy your customers—surprise them.

8. Be professional. Your only option as a sales entrepreneur is to be guided by a professional code of conduct: walk the talk. It is critical that your verbal presentation be in sync with your visual presentation. That means sound professional and look professional. Don't show up looking like a bum but sounding like a pro, or vice versa. Also, use professional language, don't swear or use slang. Even if your customer is using colorful superlatives, don't lower yourself. Maintain a level of conduct that says you are a professional, a true sales entrepreneur. Yes, be yourself, but don't engage in activity or conversation that erodes your credibility or your professional conduct. Also, be consistent. Customers are sceptical and suspicious of inconsistent behavior. You have worked hard to get to the presentation stage. Don't blow it by being inconsistent throughout the sales process. The Sequential Model demands professional consistency at every step—no missing pieces.

9. Take the customer to the presentation. Rather than struggling to take all your stuff to your customers, it can be easier and a bit more exciting to take your customers out of the office on a field trip. Take them on a tour of your facility or perhaps show them your product already in use at one of your other customers' locations. I have known salespeople who have flown potential customers to tour their head office and meet the president and some of the personnel who will be involved in servicing them. Once again, most people are visual, so take advantage of that and *show* them anytime you get the chance. It's worth the trip and the investment.

This approach also communicates pride and clearly demonstrates your commitment to the relationship as well as the conviction that your solution is right for them.

10. Action plan. Don't limit your role to that of a presenter. As an entrepreneur you are there to present an entire package, which includes a next step—an action plan. Don't finish with, "Thanks for having me in. I'll call you next week." Ask for feedback, then determine a specific call to action. This could be a specific day and time to follow up, an appointment for a follow-up visit, a tour, a meeting with the design people, and so on. Don't leave empty handed.

Managing Objections: Friend or Foe?

"If only my customers would quit raising objections, selling would be a lot easier." No doubt this statement reflects the thoughts of many sales representatives, especially those with limited experience. One thing is certain about objections: they have a nasty habit of popping out of nowhere during the sales call. They can appear anywhere, at any time, and usually without warning. Nothing strikes fear in a sales representative's eyes faster than an unexpected objection.

Selling today involves an array of sophisticated skills. Many sales experts agree that the "moment of truth" of closing won't happen until you have listened to, understood, and successfully resolved any objections the customer has. Overcoming objections is your ticket to sales success—the gold medal.

Objections are strange things. Most objections are really questions or concerns *in disguise.* They are often smoke screens protecting the customer against possible buyer's remorse or the wrath of management for making a wrong purchasing decision. Although the customer may be totally honest and sincere, you may not clearly understand what the concern is.

Sales representatives view objections as the enemy, as traps that customers set to sabotage the sale and get rid of them. Sales representatives feel challenged by objections because they require an on-the-spot, unrehearsed response possibly derailing their well-rehearsed, canned pitch. You never know what the customer might object to or challenge you about. However, objections are an integral part of the whole business of selling.

Without objections, you'd be just an order-taker. The career opportunities for professional order-takers are dismal and the pay is about the same.

I suggest that well-prepared sales entrepreneurs anticipate and welcome objections. They have learned the value of objections and view them as a friend, an *ally* to the conversation. This means that managing objections should be planned for, just as with any other step of your Sequential Model. Rather than regard an objection as an obstacle, regard it as an asset to the sale. It depends on your *attitude*. Even though objections tend to sound like verbal attacks, you can't afford to have your response sound defensive or confrontational. With a positive attitude you're more likely to respond without any hint of hostility, which makes your customer more receptive. A positive attitude can be communicated by use of a cushioning statement, an empathy statement, such as: "You're right, our price is higher than most, but what exactly is your concern?" This helps build rapport and encourages trust. Remember, it is your reaction to the objection that counts, not the objection itself.

Give some thought as to how you view objections. How do you respond to objections? What's your attitude? You're on the right track if, upon hearing an objection, your immediate response is to ask yourself, "What exactly does the customer mean by that?" If there's any doubt, and often there is (don't assume), simply clarify the concern in one of these ways:

- What do you mean by that?
- Is this what you mean?
- Tell me more.
- Please elaborate.
- I'm not sure I understand.

The cardinal rule for managing objections is: Never offer a response to an objection until you fully understand how it relates to this particular customer and this particular situation.

The cause of objections is somewhat universal. It's an uneasiness brought on by unsatisfied, unanswered, or undeveloped expectations. Remove the cause of an objection and you remove the concern. Objections may stem from political reasons (my sister works for your competitor), personal biases (I prefer to deal with XYZ company), or from prejudices (I've heard bad things about your company). Most, however, come from unsatisfied personal or corporate expectations. The probing skills developed in Chapter 7 will help you explore customer expectations. We all feel uneasy about purchasing something that hasn't dealt with all of our concerns and expectations, voiced or unvoiced. It's impossible to effectively anticipate all possible objections. Objections are as varied as customers themselves. I suggest you develop strategies (responses) for the more common objections you may encounter.

However, objections are good barometers for the sales call. They show your customer is listening and they provide a means of clarification while stimulating conversation. Simply consider objections as *conversational speed bumps,* slowing you down long enough to grasp what the customer's concerns are. Look at each objection as a spotlight on a particular concern. Once satisfactorily resolved, each grants you the right to advance the sale. Objections are also a means for customers to direct the conversation in line with their expectations. They offer a huge communication advantage. Rather than you yacking aimlessly (feature dumping), customer objections provide navigational signposts guiding you where the conversation needs to go. It helps both of you stay in sync and helps shrink the sales cycle. The absence—not the presence—of objections should be cause for concern. One of the surest signs of a bad or deteriorating relationship is the absence of objections. The customer is either bored, not being candid, or is simply not interested.

It is important, however, to draw a distinction between objections and tough questions. The difference can be significant, yet subtle. Objections are expressed in *response* to a comment or information you provided. A tough question is asked to *retrieve* information from you. Treat the tough question as just that, a question to gain new information. Be straightforward and provide specific information that directly answers the question. For example, the customer might raise an objection right after you bridged a feature, challenging you to further validate the benefit, whereas a tough question may deal with a potentially difficult situation that many salespeople mistakenly interpret as an objection. The customer will either be satisfied with your answer, ask another question, or generate a new objection. In either case, know the difference and employ the appropriate response.

Five-Step Strategy

Let's look at an appropriate response to managing objections, guided by the five-step strategy.

1. Acknowledge and validate your customers' objections. Don't stick your head in the sand and hope they go away or the customer forgets about them. Even postponement of the objection may result in a negative perception or reaction from your customer. Some sales seminars have suggested that it is best to ignore the objection, that it's only important if the customer brings it up more than once. Wrong. The next time they think of it may be after you've left and your competitor is in the customer's office, more than happy to address the very objection you ignored. Show respect and empathy by immediately acknowledging the concern. Simply say, "Yes, I can understand your concern," or, "Other customers initially felt the same way," or, "That's a fairly common concern in our business. I will be happy to address it." Remember, always express empathy and sincerity, and never get defensive. Watch your nonverbal responses as well. Turn the objections into positives by regarding them as gateways into your customer's thought process. Objections are really just your customer voicing concerns and explaining primary expectations and needs. Be sure to *hear between the lines*. Take the time to think about what is being said and the way it is being said. Sales representatives too often leap on an objection before the customer has had a chance to finish talking. The customer barely gets ten words out and the sales representative is already hammering away at a defensive response: "I have to show he's mistaken, how could he be so misinformed?" It's a panicky reaction that often sabotages the sale and the relationship. The best defense is a good, professional offense.

2. **Clarify your customer's specific objection.** Paraphrase with questions that help you understand the objection. Though some customers are adept at voicing needs as needs, others voice their needs as objections. All objections can be used to your advantage, once you realize that you are gaining valuable information.

Identify their objection as either *factual,* based on logic, or *emotional,* based on personal perception and biases. Objections are usually motivated by one or the other. Factual objections are much easier to deal with because incorrect information or incorrect perceptions can be corrected. Facts are objective, universal, and inarguable. Emotional objections, however, are extremely difficult to deal with. They are subjective and often merely an excuse or smoke screen. They usually don't follow sound reasoning and may take patience and persistence to overcome. They sometimes conceal a hidden concern that you may never be privy to. Once again, effective use of conversational probes will eventually get you to the root cause of the objection. As you ask questions, stay relaxed, listen carefully (take notes) and appreciate that you're about to learn something important. As a last resort, the eventual resolution may have to be to flag it as a C account and move on.

3. Respond to the objection immediately and solve the problem. It represents the customer's predominant thought at the moment, so make it yours. Remember, your customer is probably expressing legitimate corporate curiosity, not launching a personal attack on you.

Satisfying the customer's objection or concern may be as simple as mentally scrolling down your menu of features and presenting the one that will eliminate the objection. The "feel-felt-found" method is an effective strategy to manage objections. The sequence is important and should sound like this: "I can understand how you *feel* . . . other customers *felt* the same way . . . but once onboard with us this is what they *found* . . ." Provide details about how other customers benefited from their decision to buy from you. A testimonial letter may strengthen your case. You can actually demonstrate that other customers realized their initial opinions were unfounded after they tried your product. This is an excellent method, especially for Socializers and Relators because they tend to care what other people think.

4. Validate that the objection has been satisfied. Don't assume that you have satisfied the customer's concern. There is nothing worse than plowing through the sale, leaving behind unresolved, unanswered objections. If you don't resolve them, your competitor will.

To validate acceptance of your response, simply ask the customer, "Have I satisfied your concern?" By answering yes, the customer grants you permission to carry on with the sale. A no answer may indicate that further clarification is necessary.

5. Uncover objections up front. Sales entrepreneurs know that certain features of their product or service may be vulnerable to the competition. Although not all objections can be preempted, the more common ones can be addressed during the conversation. Bring it up *before* the customer does. A sales entrepreneur may approach the price issue by saying: "Other customers have expressed concern that our product is expensive. Well, let me show you the true value in relation to the cost." You now go on to bridge the appropriate features to benefits. Customers have no need to raise objections already stated and answered by the salesperson. This strategy will help thwart possible false or shallow objections that may stall the sale. Try to eliminate tough objections early in the conversation for an objection-free close at the end. A fun example of this strategy: Next time you're feeling frisky, take two aspirin and a glass of water up to bed. Ask your spouse to take the two pills. Of course she will ask what they are. When you tell her they are aspirin she'll probably say, "But I don't have a headache." Great!

The Price Objection

When was the last time you made a purchase solely based on price? You haven't and I doubt you ever will. Your customers don't either. Yes, I certainly agree that price is very important, but it's usually six or seven down the list of importance. Variables within the purchasing decision that may precede price include size, color, delivery, warranties, availability, after-sales service, quantities, terms and conditions, and so on.

Price objections are the easiest and most common—they have become a very natural and predictable part of the call. Sales entrepreneurs expect them. It's as if customers have been trained or conditioned to raise the price objection during every sales call. Part of the problem is that the retail community bombards us with advertisements and promotions focusing on price. We've all heard "We won't be undersold," or "Our price is the lowest, it's the law," or "If you find it cheaper we will pay you twice the difference." Every time you pick up the newspaper, read flyers, see TV commercials, listen to the radio, or stroll through your local mall, it's PRICE PRICE PRICE. No wonder when we arrive at our customers' offices they scream, "WHAT'S YOUR BEST PRICE?" Simply respond by politely asking your customer to refrain from watching TV commercials, reading newspapers, or listening to the radio ever again. It seems to be more of a conditioned, automatic response than a legitimate concern.

"You get what you pay for." This cliché has been around for decades but the message seems to be overlooked by some customers. There will always be customers who have convinced themselves that a low price is their number one priority. However, my sense is that more and more customers are appreciating that price is only one small component of the sale. To support my point, I share with you a comment from economist John Ruskin.

> It's unwise to pay too much . . . but it's worse to pay too little. When you pay too much, you lose a little money . . . that is all. When you pay too little, you sometimes lose everything, because the thing you bought was incapable of doing the

thing it was bought to do. The common law of business balance prohibits paying a little and getting a lot—it can't be done. If you deal with the lowest bidder, it is well to add something for the risk you run. And if you do that, you will have enough to pay for something better.

John   Ruskin
1819–1900

What impresses me is this was written before 1900. The rationale underlying his theory hasn't changed in 100 years.

Zig Ziglar offers this explanation in support of a competitive price: "Our company made the decision to explain a higher price *once* rather than justify poor service and quality several times." Great line. I tell my students, "You only cry once when you pay a higher price."

What is a competitive price? Research tells us that customers will pay 8% to 12% more for perceived value. Customers will put their money where their mouth is if you deliver a value-added solution—but anything over 12% and the customer may resist. For example, if your competition is priced at $1,000 you can charge $1,120 and still be considered competitively priced ($1,000 + 12%). Anything above the 12% may be too aggressive. Hence, your objective is not to match your competition at the $1,000 price but rather to price it higher due to the value you created. As a consumer, I'm sure that on more than one occasion you paid a higher price because you appreciated the service and attention you received. Your customers are no different.

The best advice I can offer is that price should not be discussed during the Discovery or Confirming steps of your Sequential Model. Price is an issue you *negotiate*. Don't sell it. What I mean by "selling it" is that salespeople often try to confirm the sale by focusing the conversation on a discounted price.

Sell a *value-added* solution during the call, not a price solution. Don't make price the focal point of the call. I discuss price in more detail in Chapter 10, Negotiation Skills.

Understand the difference between price objection and price resistance. Price objection is a matter of clear opposition to your price—I can't pay it, or I won't pay it because we have limited funds, and so on. Price resistance suggests your customers have the capacity to withstand or tolerate your price. They may not like it initially, but they will pay it. Salespeople often respond to price resistance by immediately offering to lower it. Wrong thing to do. Try to focus on building value instead of reducing the price. Rarely is the sale based solely on price, so don't become an order-taker, getting the sale on little more than your good looks and a cheap price. Customers buy based on their perceptions of the overall value you present. So, how do you create a high perceived value? I think William Brooks answers that question succinctly in his book, *Niche Selling*. He offers the following formula where V is value, PB is perceived benefits, and PP is perceived price:[3]

$$V = \frac{PB}{PP}$$

This formula clearly shows that the higher the PB, the higher the value: V increases as PB increases and PP decreases. For example; if we have a PP weighting of 10 and a PB weighting of only 5, then V=0.5. However, if we inverse the numbers where PB=10 and PP=5, our V=2. The first example where V=0.5 tells us that the focus was on price (PP=10). Our second example, where V=2, the focus was on selling benefits, thus V was four times greater than in the first example. The key to increase the PB is to focus on bridging the appropriate features to the benefits, as we discussed in Chapter 7.

Next time your customer says, "Yes, but what's your best price?" this is what he really means; "You did a good job here today Bernie. That was the best feature dump I've seen this week. However, you have failed to sell me anything of value so I have no option but to create value myself. The only way I can do that is by hammering you on price. If I get you down low enough, then maybe I'll see some value and buy from you." When you fail to create value, your customer tries to do it by way of a low-low price. Not a good way to sell. As one sales manager said, "The day we are the cheapest price is the day we sell this stuff by direct mail." Let's stop this order-taking stuff and focus on selling true value to our customers.

Consider this: When you pitch features, telling versus selling, the customer sets the price. When you present benefits, a value-added solution, you set the price. It's your choice.

Bring It Forward

Another common situation involves the stall objection or the timing objection. A customer may say: "Sounds good but we can't look at it until the next quarter or our next fiscal year. Call me in six months." The timing may not be good or they need to stall until a new budget becomes available. My strategy in these situations is to *bring it forward*—bring the situation forward as if the customer were making a decision today. Simply invite the customer to enter into the *hypothetical arena* and ask, "Hypothetically, if you were to consider making a decision today, what would you be looking for? What's important to you?" Maximize this opportunity with the customer, do a mini-discovery to learn some initial criteria for when it comes time to make a decision. You then provide a mini-presentation, giving your customer some insight into what your solution can offer. If your customer is receptive and sees value, ask him or her a hypothetical close, "If you were to make a decision today, would you buy from me?" Remember, reiterate to the customer that this is all hypothetical so by no means are they making a commitment. By going through this *bring it forward* strategy, you and your customer know there is valid reason to take a serious look at you come decision time.

This strategy far outweighs the alternative, which is to say to your customer: "Okay fine, I understand you won't be looking at this for six months. I'll call you then." Don't leave yourself vulnerable to the competition. Secure an initial commitment by using the *bring it forward* strategy and you may pique the customer's interest enough that he looks forward to having a serious conversation with you at the appropriate time. Heck, he may even say to your competitors, "Thanks for calling but we're already looking at somebody."

Your overall objective is to deliver a creative, value-added solution that leaves no doubt in the customer's mind that you're the best solution. Make a vivid impression with an innovative, convincing presentation. Cookie-cutter, boring presentations do little to advance the sale—customers buy differences, not similarities.

Don't overlook the *you* solution. Your competitor may offer similar products or services with competitive pricing, but they can't duplicate you. Next time you're asked the question, "Why should I buy from you?" look the customer square in the eyes and say, "Because I'm your salesperson." Don't depend on a product solution or a price solution to differentiate yourself. Your greatest asset is yourself.

NOTES

1. Wilson, Larry. *Changing the Game: The New Way to Sell*. Page 81, 1987. Simon & Schuster Inc..

2. Decker, Bert. *You've Got to Be Believed to Be Heard: Reach The First Brain to Communicate in Business and In Life*. Page 84, 1992. St. Martin's Press.

3. Brooks, William T. *Niche Selling: How to Find Your Customer in a Crowded Market.*. Page 28, 1992. Business One Irwin.

Congratulations, you have now completed
Step #6

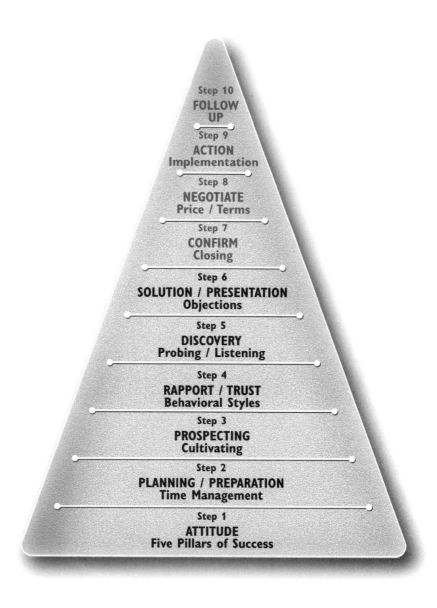

Chapter 9

CONFIRMING
THE SALE: CLOSING

People buy from people. Better yet, people love to buy. The buying experience can be very rewarding and can satisfy many of the motives to buy: ego, prestige, status, greed, joy of spending money, peace of mind, and so on. The ideal sales process is a mutual journey of honesty, trust, and respect as you and your customer work in harmony through the Sequential Model. When the journey is mutual, confirming the sale is not a matter of *if*, but *when*.

Traditionally, this step is referred to as "closing the sale." However, the word "closing" has negative connotations that conjure up images of unscrupulous sales representatives using manipulative, guerrilla tactics designed to coerce unsuspecting customers into buying. Traditional closing techniques typically violate the sales relationship. Customers today are tired and irritated by these offensive, manipulative, unethical arm-twisting tactics.

Make buying easy for your customer by *confirming* the sale using a nonmanipulative, straightforward approach and presenting a practical, value-added solution. Confirming is the pinnacle of selling achievement. It is when the customer awards a gold medal to the salesperson who delivered a win-win, value-added performance. However, confirming does not happen in isolation from the total sales process. You need to be *engineering commitment* throughout the entire sales call because anything you do or say, at any step, will either erode or enhance the sale. Chronologically, the confirmation comes as Step #7 of the Sequential Model, but be cognizant that your success at this point is based on a *series* of buy-ins or confirmations through-out the journey. Confirmation simply means to create a shared sense of enthusiasm to do business then exercise the *power of asking.* The ideal situation is a sales entrepreneur who can con-fidently ask for the business and at the same time be diligent in building a relationship by asking smart questions. Don't under-estimate the power of asking.

> "Man who wait for roast duck to fly into mouth,
> wait very, very long time."
>
> *Chinese Proverb*

Why is it that so many salespeople become paralyzed with fear at the thought of *closing?* Even when they have successfully navigated through the previous six steps they still fail to ask for a buying decision. The reasons are as diverse as customers them-selves. The most common one is *fear.* Fear of rejection, fear of sounding silly, fear of failure, fear of upsetting the customer, the feeling of not being good enough or worthy enough to ask. All valid reasons, but unfortunately this becomes a negative habit pattern that seriously compromises our success at confirming. In the interest of harmony and not offending a potential customer, we unknowingly sacrifice our own agendas by failing to ask.

Psychologists agree that the fear of asking is learned through negative conditioning experienced as early as childhood. Our parents, teachers, siblings, and even friends have all contributed to nurturing this debilitating virus. No one is born with it. Your fears are all learned and reinforced through repetition by those around you, even yourself. As one lady said when finally asked out by a fellow she admired, "The trouble with you men is that you often reject yourselves before you give us women a chance to." She was elated when he finally asked her out, and without hesitation accepted his invitation. The same analogy applies to salespeople. We often reject or doubt our own proposals or presentations long before we give the customer a chance to. However, because it is a learned condition, it can be unlearned as well, and sometimes very quickly. I suggest there is a direct relationship between low corporate self-esteem and negative self-talk, and your confidence to ask for business. Confirming demands an attitude of confidence, *expecting* the customer to say yes. Anything less puts you in entrepreneurial quicksand. Just as the Chinese proverb suggests, don't expect rewards such as roast duck or a confirmed sale unless you ASK.

Five Magic Words

Okay then, how do I confirm the sale? The Sequential Model offers a refreshingly simple approach to confirming. In fact, the apparent simplicity of it usually invites suspicion. "That's it, it's that simple?" Let me give you the five most powerful words you'll ever say when working through your Sequential Model. Look your customer square in the eyes, and with all the confidence you can muster say these five magic words . . . . .

"May I have your business?"

—and don't say another thing until the customer has responded.

That's it! Five words. So simple that I dedicated an entire page to them. These words reflect clarity, sincerity, innocence, and professionalism. Go ahead, put the book down and say them aloud. Say them again. These five words are applicable to all four behavioral styles. Any one of the four styles will appreciate the intent and clarity of your question.

As you can clearly see, your Sequential Model need not rely on clever closing gimmicks to trick people into buying something they don't want. The beauty of this approach is that you know what you are saying, and the customer knows what you are asking. Forget about memorizing 50 different power closes—keep it simple.

What often sabotages this clean, refreshing approach is the confusion generated by the numerous books available on closing skills. Many of them, by title alone, suggest the need to build an inventory of closing techniques. Some books even suggest "The more closes you know, the better you're prepared to face the moment of truth." Nonsense. Consider this passage taken from Dartnell's publication, *Close It Right, Right Now!:*

> Contrary to the popular belief that closing is an "end-game," or a final manipulation that sparks agreement, closing is a constant and continuing activity. I warm to the salesperson who shows interest in me. That helps me decide in his or her favor. I am attracted by a sales presentation that gives me clear information. That helps me favor that product. I appreciate learning about how the product fits my needs and benefits me. That helps me exclude other products I may have considered.
>
> In the absence of all those good things, I am not likely to buy, no matter how clever the salesperson is in trying to button up the sale. In fact, I am driven from closing when I perceive too much cleverness in the procedure.[1]

I have seen numerous books outlining countless closing techniques, all advocating the need to have a ready supply of closes to apply when needed, and all suggesting that an inventory of closes is directly related to your success. One such publication goes so far as to offer: "Twenty-Nine Special Closings That Rock Holdouts and Crack Hardcases."[2] Another publication, *The Sales Closing Book,* offers "more than 270 powerful sales closes that can skyrocket your sales and income." The ultimate prize for trickery goes to a publication that offers this gem: "35 Tactics for Psychological Manipulation: The Master Closer's Mind Game List."[3] Some typical closes include:

The Whispering Close	The Blitz	The Airplane Close
The Half-Nelson	Lost Sale Close	Extra Incentive Close
Ego/Profit Close	P.O.W. Story	Conditional Close
Puppy Dog Demo	The Silent Close	Callback Close
The Columbo Close	Return Serve Close	The Negative Close
Door Knob Close	The Grind	Emotional Close
Mutt and Jeff	Last Resort Close	Assumption Close

Imagine the mental gymnastics required to sort through all those memorized "closes" to decide which one to use. Unbelievable! I think the only thing that will skyrocket will be your level of stress and anxiety.

Once again, the entrepreneurial sales call should be a dialogue, a conversation between two human beings. Forget about memorized closings, putting cute names on closing techniques, or rehearsed scripts. These memorized closes are often manipulative, guerrilla approaches that compensate for not being good.

Customers like to be asked and they respect the salesperson who asks for their business in an honest, confident, nonmanipulative manner. However, research suggests that in approximately 70% of sales calls, there is never a direct request for the business. It may seem like an unbelievable statistic given that confirming is the final effort of a gold-medal performance (second place is the first loser), but it's true. Many salespeople attempt to confirm the sale but end up skirting the issue with a weak, unconvincing request to do business. A common attempt at confirming sounds like this:

S: Is there anything else I can show you or answer for you today?

C: No, thank you. You've answered all my questions and I have all the information I need.

S: Okay then. Well, let me leave you with our most recent brochure and a copy of my presentation. Mr. Smith, let me ask you, are you available next week?

C: Yes, I expect to be around.

S: Great. Why don't I give you a call early next week and we can discuss my proposal further and see how you feel about it. Is that okay?

C: Sure, that's fine.

S: Great. Thanks for your time.

A classic unsuccessful close. The salesperson has avoided asking a direct question to buy and is leaving with nothing more than hope and a sense of accomplishment. Of course, in the meantime, the salesperson is totally vulnerable to the prey of the competition. As coincidence would have it, the competition shows up the very next day offering the customer the same solution, but the difference is that she exercised the power of asking. She wins the gold, the salesperson wins nothing more than experience. I implore you to safeguard yourself against the competition and reevaluate your confirming tactics. No customer, at least that I'm aware of, will ever reward you for just showing up and making a good sales pitch. Ask yourself: Is my confirmation a direct invitation to purchase? Is it clean, honest, direct, and nonmanipulative? Test it out on fellow sales entrepreneurs, your sales manager, or your mentor.

Tim Commandment #6
Confirm the sale with a direct, simple question. Ask: Did I ask for their business?

Now, before you unceremoniously discount my confirming theory, appreciate that I'm only suggesting this approach (the five words) in the interest of simplicity, honesty, and the power of asking. I recognize that there are other tactics to confirming. In fact, I endorse more than one approach. For example, simply ask your customer, "Since we both appear to be in agreement, what's *our* next step?" or alternatively ask, "Where do we go from here?" You can preface this confirmation question with a summary statement outlining the accepted benefits.

Is It No, or Is It Know?

Time for a spelling lesson. It's important to understand the difference between *no* and *know.* Sales representatives spell no as *no,* taking the meaning literally as more rejection, another opportunity lost. (But of course you can't lose something you never had.) Conversely, sales entrepreneurs spell no as *know:* the customer simply needs to *know* more information before making a positive buying decision. It's not interpreted as rejection but more as an invitation to explain the possible benefits of doing business. By saying *know,* the customer has not yet seen the value in your offering and needs to *know* more about your tailored solution. This means going back to feature fishing and scrolling your corporate menu for appropriate features (hot-buttons), then bridging to create a benefit package worthy of consideration. That's value. Upon hearing a *know,* you might consider asking the customer: "What is the single barrier preventing us from moving forward?" A candid response may spotlight a potential objection that when managed effectively produces a yes. Until the customer sees value, you'll continue to hear *knows.*

Remember, earlier in the book I defined selling as the process of disruption. Making a change in suppliers or adding a new supplier to the list is scary at the best of times. Customers experience fear and anxiety just as we do. Your benefit package has to be convincing enough to disrupt customers into change. Customers will continue to say *know* if there is a bigger yes offered by the competition.

Three Ingredients of a Yes

Just as a good fire needs three ingredients to burn, so does a successful confirmation. Take away any one of the three ingredients and you have no fire, no sale. The three ingredients of a Yes are: rapport, trust, and the power of asking. Just as with the five rights of passage in our definition of selling, you can't take away or fail to establish any one of the three. Unfortunately, many salespeople create rapport and trust comfortably, but fail to ask a direct, honest, confirming question. Sometimes they do ask, but have failed to first create rapport or trust. Would a customer give you a bag of money if he trusted you but you failed to ask? Not likely. Would he say yes if he didn't like you or trust you? Not likely. It's all part of engineering commitment. You start confirming the sale the second you come in contact, by telephone or otherwise, with your potential customer.

I find it amusing to hear the different excuses as to why a customer didn't buy. Sales representatives are the best "fire-dancers" on the planet. Each probably has 50 excuses, all conveniently memorized, and of course none blame themselves. During my years as a sales manager, I could have written a book on. "The reasons why I didn't get the sale." No doubt it would have challenged David Chilton's book, *The Wealthy Barber*, as an international all-time best seller. I offer only one reason why a salesperson didn't get the sale and ended up in second place. My reason doesn't make me popular but it's inarguable: "You didn't get the business because you were *outsold*." Pure and simple. Strip away all the excuses and that's what's left. The customer had a need and a bag of money and decided to give it to your competitor. Why? Your competitor probably offered a better, value-added solution having asked, better, smarter questions.

When to Confirm

When does one confirm the sale? When have you earned the right to ask this most feared and sacred question? The answer remains elusive, subject to broad interpretation, often founded on your interpretation of perceived buying signals. The majority of sales literature suggests confirming, "When the prospect is ready and communicates a buying signal," or, "When the buyer appears ready." I have always marvelled at the ambiguity in terms of when to confirm. Several authors suggest that you rely on little more than your own perception of body language and discrete buying signals to interpret when they're ready to buy. Unless body language or buying signals are very obvious, you run the risk of misinterpreting the customer's nonverbal communication. I agree that body language is a powerful component of the communication model, but not as the sole method of interpreting when to close. Everyone is different, just as behavioral flexibility suggests, each individual has a unique body-language style (Chapter 6). Socializers adapt their body language differently from Directors but they could be thinking the same thing. I don't think that we can apply a universal set of standards to effectively and accurately interpret body language.

When discussing body language at my seminars, I often notice a participant leaning back in his or her chair with arms folded. I ask the participant not to move and point out their posture to the class. The class usually agrees that the school of body language would have us interpret that posture as detached, uninterested, and guarded. I then validate my theory by asking the participant with folded arms, "Are you comfortable?" The answer, not surprisingly, is usually, "Yes." My suggestion is not to concern yourself with body language unless it's obvious or unless there is a drastic change during the sales call. Let your customer be comfortable without interpreting posture as a negative buying signal. The only real body language that I respond to is if my customer gets up and leaves the office. Then I clue in that perhaps the call isn't going as well as I'd hoped.

So, when do you confirm the sale? Confirm the sale when you have successfully bridged a minimum of *two* features to benefits. You have now earned the right to ask. One bridged benefit is usually not enough to convince them to buy, which is why I suggest a minimum of two. If the customer says yes, that's great. Go to Step #8. If they say *know*, then go back to feature fishing and continue to bridge. As we can appreciate, each customer is different. Some only require two benefits to confirm, others may require several. Once again, customers may simply need to *know* more before they say yes.

Nine Tips for Confirming the Sale

1. Ask a confirming question only after you have effectively bridged a minimum of two appropriate features to benefits.

2. Help people make buying decisions by pointing out how your value-added solution will benefit their business.

3. Highlight how the benefits outweigh the costs; create value.

4. Successful confirmation isn't an isolated tactic, it's creating value throughout the Sequential Model.

5. If you can't confirm, you didn't successfully complete a prior step—planning, discovery, or presenting a creative, value-added solution.

6. Before asking for a decision, expect customers to say yes—mentally picture them saying it.

7. When you ask people for a buying decision, be quiet until they respond.

8. A confirming question asks for a decision. A trial close such as, "What do you think of my presentation so far?" calls for an opinion.

9. If you can't make a sale, make a friend.

Doubling Your Close Ratio

Recall that approximately 80% of purchases occur after the order has been requested five times and yet only 10% of salespeople ask five times before quitting. Likewise, 40% of salespeople ask only once, then quit. These 40% quit for a variety of reasons: impatience, the craving for instant gratification, poor follow-up, no time-management system, or just simple laziness.

There is no doubt that these statistics are shocking, but customers are the victims of these lackluster performances on a daily basis.

Imagine having to confirm five times before you get a yes. That means, on average, there are four *knows* before a yes. That's a lot of work! Some authors suggest selling is a numbers game: talk to ten people, get five presentations, close two deals. That sounds like a lot of work—not selling very smart. It bears out the fact that the average close ratio is only 20%. That means, on average, salespeople close only two out of ten potential opportunities. Funny, I always thought selling was about people, not a game with winners, losers, and average, mediocre performances. Don't fall victim to the numbers game, condemning your career to a life of mediocrity. Don't measure your success against the masses. By comparing yourself against the averages, you only fuel a false sense of productivity. I say set your own standards. Don't take pride in being average—it's too easy and not very satisfying.

Remember that confirming is not an event but a process that begins within minutes of meeting the customer. Customers are very quick to pass judgment, wasting no time deciding if you are likable and trustworthy. The first step to doubling your close ratio is to

ensure the first six steps of your sequential model have been completed to the customer's satisfaction.

Hence, if close ratios are a meager 20% that means the customers' ratio is 80%. Ouch! Customers are closing more often than we are. They sell us on the concept of not doing business with them. They offer a multitude of excuses, objections, and justifications all in the interest of selling us their "no." The problem is we are too quick to accept their rejection and with a bruised ego return to the adult day-care center to lick our wounds and seek support. Sound familiar?

So, what is a good close ratio? I would suggest that as a sales entrepreneur your target should be no less than 40–50%. That means if you approach ten potential customers, ones with a need and a bag of money, you should confirm at least four to five. Sound daunting? It isn't. Some top-notch sales entrepreneurs are confirming up to 75% of potential customers.

Start by evaluating your current ratio. Track it for a month or two and reality will quickly reveal itself. It may not be as high as you think it is. If yours is higher than 20%, congratulations, you are in the minority. But I will remind you, your objective is 40–50%. Proper execution of your Sequential Model will certainly contribute to doubling your current close ratio. It simply means building rapport and trust as you navigate through the first six steps of your model coupled with the confidence to ask for their business. Customers expect to be asked; don't disappoint them. They get irritated by reps who fail to complete the sales call with no direct close. You represent a solution to their needs, so the only outstanding issue is to ask them. If you don't someone else will—and be rewarded with a bag of money. Hence, taking your close ratio to 40% is not an impossible, arduous objective.

However, I caution you, don't strive to achieve a 100% confirmation ratio. Not only will it never happen, you don't want 100%. You couldn't handle it. You're already time-starved with what you have. Free up time by firing C accounts (and C activities) and increase productivity by doubling your confirmation ratio on A and B opportunities. If a 100% confirmation ratio is your goal, then work at McDonalds or Burger King. Everyone who walks in buys something. When was the last time you heard this conversation in McDonald's:

"May I help you?"

"Oh, no thanks, just looking."

My point is this: Achieving a confirmation ratio of 50% is hard work, and yet it can be very rewarding. Success is hard work. A job that has a 100% confirmation ratio generally pays minimum wage.

Be #2

When it comes time to confirm, you will certainly encounter customers who say no, and mean no. Don't despair. An excellent alternative plan is to have your customers place a small order with you. Tell them you are not expecting them to make a wholesale change in suppliers, but ask them to place a small order to test you out. The proof is in the pudding. It's okay to be #2, just ask the people at AVIS Rent-a-Car. If you are successful at getting and delivering a few small orders, it won't be long before you build up to getting the lion's share of their business. Chances are your unsuspecting competitor won't know what happened until it's too late. I have personally converted several accounts from a *no* to a *know* to a *yes* by using this strategy. Customers can be creatures of habit and usually go with what's been tested and proven. Your #2 strategy provides an opportunity to showcase your stuff while building confidence and trust in you. Remember, the fifth pillar of success is Patient yet Persistent (Chapter 2). Quiet persistence, coupled with patience, ultimately pay off handsomely with the reward of becoming their #1 supplier.

Always act like a professional. Don't take the customer's rejection personally. Recognize it as a business decision based on circumstances you may be unaware of. Be grateful for the opportunity to meet and discuss the possibility of doing business. The professional handling of a *no sale* situation actually helps build a sound relationship by developing a spirit of professionalism and persistence. The customer will be much more receptive to a #2 strategy if you handle the no sale situation professionally. Remember, if you can't make a sale, make a friend.

One of the greatest pleasures of selling is the adrenaline rush and elation when the customer says, "Yes, let's do business." This is the *moment of yes.* There have been many private dances in customer's parking lots, clenched fists pumping through the air accompanied by triumphant shouts of, "Yesss!" and smiles that make dentists proud. Confirming the sale is the pinnacle of achievement—all your efforts have paid a handsome return. Unquestionably, the greatest thrill for a sales entrepreneur is the moment of yes when the customer agrees to buy from you in the interest of a honest, mutually beneficial solution.

Become comfortable with using the five magic words and make them part of your professional equity. Confirming with these five words communicates confidence and offers a refreshing change for the customer. Another tremendous advantage is that this approach is universal—the same five words can be used regardless of what you are selling. Big-ticket items, long sales cycles, short sales cycles, a product or service, it doesn't matter—

the five words must be applied to every possible sales scenario. Sales entrepreneurs understand that the power of asking is what ultimately separates a professional salesperson from a professional *conversationalist*.

NOTES

1. The Editors at Dartnell. Dartnell's Professional Selling Series Volume 2: *Close It Right, Right Now: How to Close More Sales Fast*. Page 3, 1995. The Dartnell Corporation.

2. Roth, Charles B. & Roy Alexander. *Secrets of Closing Sales*. Page 209, 1993. Prentice Hall.

3. Pickens, James W. *The Art of Closing Any Deal: How to be a "Master Closer" In Everything You Do*. Page 91, 1991. Warner Books.

Congratulations, you have now completed
Step #7

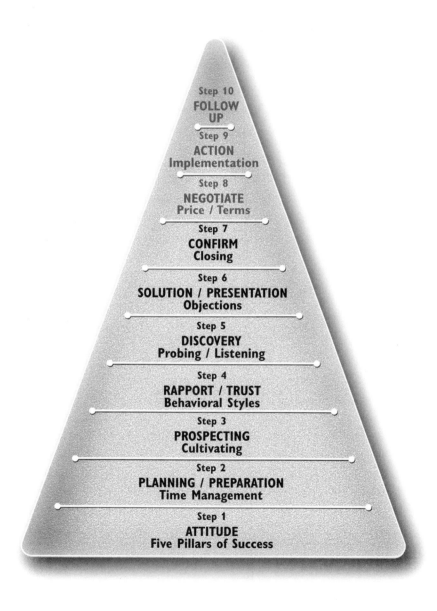

Chapter 10

CREATIVE NEGOTIATION: THERE IS ALWAYS A WAY

Children are accomplished negotiators. If they need extra allowance, a later bedtime, a sleepover, they usually get it. Children can be relentless in their pursuit of what they want. Familiarity gives them the advantage of knowing what parental hot-buttons to push. They are the best examples of ideal negotiators. Then they grow up and abandon the natural negotiating talents they learned instinctively.

Like selling, negotiation is something we use in every facet of our lives. I am often entertained just watching my three teenagers negotiate the use of one car. Amazingly, it usually works out. I think most of us are better negotiators than we give ourselves credit for. Negotiation is one of those transparent, interpersonal skills we use unconsciously. Negotiation is really a relationship skill used by people to deal with their conflicts and differences. Throughout this chapter, my goal is to leverage existing negotiation skills to build confidence and an awareness of long-forgotten negotiation principles and tactics.

Unfortunately, the very thought of negotiation conveys negative connotations, striking fear in the souls of most salespeople. Often the outcome of negotiation leaves people feeling dissatisfied, worn out, or alienated. A win-lose mindset has prevailed for decades. The negotiator (customer or salesperson) attempts to win important concessions and thus triumph over the opponent. It resembles the outcome of most sports: winner–loser. Not all successful salespeople are good negotiators. Most salespeople are not adequately trained in the art of negotiation and don't understand its many nuances. The necessary traits for successful negotiation vary somewhat, but some characteristics are universal, including patience, persistence, stamina, and confidence. Each negotiation is situational, with both sides discussing the points over which disagreement exists. In reality, no single negotiation session covers exactly the same issues or demands.

When Do We Negotiate?

Almost anything can be negotiated with the application of sound principles. The biggest misunderstanding is not so much how to negotiate, but when. Salespeople eager to do the deal often initiate premature negotiation, trying to negotiate before the time is right.

So, when is the best time to negotiate? In the majority of sales situations, salespeople attempt to enter into negotiation *before* the customer has agreed to do business. There is a better, more productive approach.

Sales professionals engage in negotiation when a customer has expressed an interest to do business. We negotiate *after* the confirmation step, after the customer has agreed to do business with you.

Upon initial reflection this concept may seem bizarre and contrary to traditional sales techniques, but that's only because you've done it that way for years. Although it may have worked for you in the past, it's not a very smooth or fluid approach.

Confirmation has two aspects: *initial* confirmation, where the customer is in agreement and willingly moves into the negotiation phase; and *final* confirmation, where the customer has accepted all the terms and conditions of your solution, including price. Initial confirmation may sound like this: "If we can work out a competitive price, may I have your business?" If the customer is in agreement, you now have earned the right to negotiate. It's much easier to negotiate terms, conditions, and price once you have a willing party. Your next step is final confirmation: "Now that we have agreed on a competitive price may I have your business?" It doesn't need to get any more complicated than that.

In our two-day sales negotiation seminar, salespeople are often shocked to learn that price should not be part of the sale. It's a separate discussion that takes place as part of negotiating final confirmation. It's no different than buying a house. You decide on location, size, number of bedrooms, and other features. After you pick a home you make an offer, which means you are now negotiating. The offer goes back and forth as both parties negotiate all the details, including price. In most cases the negotiating goes smoothly because there are two willing parties, a seller and a buyer. Use the same advantage in sales, by using your Sequential Model to create a willing buyer.

Tim Commandment #7
Negotiate after *initial* confirmation.
Ask: Have I earned the right to negotiate?

Now it's in each party's best interests to negotiate a win-win-win-win solution. The four winners are your customer and his or her company, and you and your company. With two willing parties there is always a way, in spite of initial barriers and disagreements. Details can be worked out when both parties are motivated to do so. If not, details can easily undermine a possible solution. It's not a good deal if one of the four wins is missing or compromised. The idea is to reach mutually beneficial agreements that resolve inconveniences or dissatisfaction and solidify long-term relationships.

Trust plays a major role in successful negotiation. Although there is no guarantee that trust will lead to collaboration, mistrust will inhibit collaboration. When people trust one another, they are more likely to communicate openly and honestly. In contrast, if people do not trust you they are more likely to withdraw and be less cooperative. Acting in a trusting manner throughout the relationship serves as an invitation to others to be trustworthy, especially if your trusting manner is consistent. Each negotiator must believe that both parties choose to behave in a cooperative manner. Trust is not a one-time, singular event. It is established over time by demonstrating professionalism, honesty, integrity, consistency, and cooperation and by following through on promises and commitments. Cooperative behavior is a signal of honesty, openness, and a shared commitment to a joint solution. Take advantage of the trust engineered throughout the first seven steps of the model. Remember, people judge us by our actions, not by our intentions.

Approaches to negotiation tend to reflect personal experiences, biases, and perceptions of the individuals involved. They are often reflected in one of two ways: *flight* or *fight*. People who take the flight approach are uncomfortable with conflict and try to avoid possible rejection, frustration, and anger associated with negotiation. They become masters at avoidance and readily prefer to take flight rather than experience any degree of conflict. Relaters tend to take the flight approach.

The fight approach is supported by a mindset of, "Only the strong survive," and "Do unto others before they do unto you."

Directors tend to favor this approach. It's a classic win–lose scenario. Bargaining and compromise are two components of fight. Bargaining is where you have a predetermined position and you haggle back and forth, working hard, grinding your opponent down. You pursue this approach until you are victorious. Compromise occurs when both sides give in and split the difference, settling for half a loaf. Compromise may satisfy both parties, but only to a limited extent. Of course, half a loaf in a highly competitive arena may be viewed as better than none but if it becomes normal practice the results may be less than desirable for both sides.

A more effective approach, one that fosters long-term relationships, is *creative* negotiation. Creative negotiation is defined as: "Both parties seek to resolve their differences by working synergistically to create a higher quality, value-added solution. Both parties acknowledge the need to reach agreement, working amicably and creatively toward a solution that satisfies each."[1]

Five Principles of Creative Negotiation

Dealing with conflict and differences is rarely an easy task. Barriers to creative negotiation can be numerous and are often the saboteurs of a potential sale. Remember: your goal is to reach win-win-win-win settlements with qualified customers. To that end, I offer these five principles of creative sales negotiation:

Principle #1: Attitude First

Are you a good negotiator? Your answer reflects your level of confidence in your negotiation skills. Creating a positive mind-set involves basic attitudinal characteristics, which become the building blocks for successful negotiation. As discussed in

Chapter 2, attitudes and skills must work in harmony. Attitudinal characteristics of negotiation include self-awareness, self-belief, and an openness to other viewpoints. Salespeople frequently overlook the importance of preparing themselves mentally. Attitude—how we deal with others when negotiating—drives the relationship. Develop a win-win-win-win attitude toward negotiation, and don't be satisfied until all parties are pleased with the solution.

Principle #2: Planning and Preparation

You may be thinking, "Dèjá vu—didn't we already discuss this?" Yes, we did, in Chapter 3. We need to talk about it again. For many of us, planning is boring and tedious, easily put off in favor of leaping into action quickly. However, devoting insufficient time to planning frequently results in failure to negotiate a mutually beneficial agreement, and raises feelings of hostility and frustration.

The cornerstone to effective, creative negotiation is a carefully designed blueprint outlining specifically desired results for both you and your customer. The first step is to clearly articulate your position—know what your objectives are. Know the issues that are not negotiable and the issues that are negotiable. I refer to them as your "must-have" and "nice-to-have" issues. Must-have issues are predetermined prior to negotiation and are essential to a satisfactory agreement. They are simply not negotiable. Your nice-to-have issues are negotiable. Although they would be nice to have, they are not essential to the agreement. They are issues you are prepared to concede or use as trade-offs in the interest of concluding the agreement or maintaining the relationship.

Your window of flexibility is guided by your predetermined min-max points—min being your lowest acceptable point and max being your best, most ideal position. So, in the interests of creative negotiation, each of your must-have issues should be accompanied by a window of flexibility—your min-max points. Let's look at the example below.

MUST-HAVE ISSUE: PROFIT
MIN-MAX POINTS

As a sales entrepreneur, your must-have issue is making a profit. To do this, you are guided by the flexibility of your pre-determined min-max points. As in Figure 10.1, the ideal situation is a max-point of $150 whereas your min-point is $100. Any price lower than your min-point is unacceptable—you may have to entertain other avenues, such as concessions or trade-offs, to secure the deal. The wider the spread between your min-max points, the more flexibility you have to negotiate. Otherwise, you may become too rigid and inflexible, deadlocking the negotiation. In terms of your nice-to-have issues, I suggest there are no min-max points. These issues are subject to negotiation and may be used as concessions to advance the deal. The key to creative negotiation is knowing your parameters *prior* to negotiation. Whenever possible, plan your strategy beforehand. It's tough to negotiate creatively if you don't know the parameters of your destination. In creative negotiation, those who ask for more typically get more . . . and those with low targets typically underachieve.

Also, consider whether negotiation is appropriate at all. It may be a C account or a C opportunity. In some sales situations negotiation can take place spontaneously, so be aware of the status of the opportunity: A, B, or C. You may have to respond on the fly so be sure to have the complete account file with you at the call for quick reference to previous discussions.

The second step in negotiation planning is to define the issues worthy of negotiation. Refer to all your notes and assemble all the issues, yours and your customer's, into a comprehensive list. Some issues may have been resolved prior to the negotiation, which is fine, but be sure to identify any outstanding issues. It can be frustrating and costly—in terms of time and success—if the customer calls you just prior to inking the deal with an unresolved issue. After the issues are assembled, the next step is to prioritize them. By sharing the list with your customer, you continue to build trust and confidence as you work through it together. Extract relevant information from your notes to enhance your position. A comment in your notes from six months ago may be a valuable piece of information. Salespeople often compensate for inadequate planning by conceding more than necessary. This shortcut can be very costly.

Sales entrepreneurs cannot afford to be quick and clever during the give and take of negotiation. Planning increases your negotiation success substantially and helps you achieve solutions that you never thought possible. Invest the time and energy (during janitorial hours) to prepare a strategy in line with your customer's behavioral style. Your strategy will help you relax, face fewer unknowns, and reduce stress.

Principle #3: Know the Lingo

The negotiation arena has a language of its own. I have seen many negotiation sessions fail simply due to not understanding the language of negotiation. My objective here is not to provide you with an in-depth study of all the nuances of negotiation but to create a mindset, an awareness, and an overview of the logistics of creative sales negotiation. I suggest you augment your negotiation skills and confidence by considering other publications on the subject. Consider this chapter as your springboard to further study.

Language of Negotiation

The following terms should become part of every sales entrepreneur's vocabulary.

1. Concessions. Giving in to a customer's request without asking for anything in return. Concessions are central to creative negotiation. They are the backbone to a mutually accepted outcome as they acknowledge the other party and communicate sensitivity to his or her issues and demands. Initial concessions can be effective—they communicate that you are willing and that your intentions are honorable. Many authors suggest that negotiation involves a "progression of concessions."

Once again, your min-max points must be clearly defined prior to giving concessions. Know your parameters and don't give away the farm. Begin the negotiation by offering small concessions. Concede the items or issues to which you attach little importance. The sooner you demonstrate your willingness to negotiate, the sooner the customer will respond in kind. Don't give away big concessions too early. Use them to respond to a customer's concession or to secure the deal: "Can we confirm the deal, if I give you XX?" However, you need to draw the line when your min-point is being compromised.

2. Trade-Offs. Give customers what they want in return for something of comparable value. Value is perception. The item may not be equal in monetary terms, but it may be equal in perceived value. As you've heard before, "One man's garbage is another man's treasure." Once again, know your must-have issues and your min-max points before determining what you are willing to trade.

The power of trade-offs is enormous and can have a tremendous impact on your productivity. By asking for a trade-off you elevate the value of your concession. It also stops the *grinding* process. Marry your concession to a trade-off, otherwise your customer will continue to make demands. You might as well say, "Sure, here you go, it's yours for the asking." A confident negotiator exercises *give* (concessions) and *take* (trade-offs) throughout the negotiation process, moving the dialogue toward a win-win-win-win solution. However, the rule of thumb is to stay flexible—there is always a way.

3. **Walk-Point.** The point where you walk away from the deal because your minimum must-have issues are not being met. If through trade-offs and concessions you are unable to reach an agreement that satisfies your predetermined parameters, your only option may be to walk. However, walking may only be a temporary solution. Both parties may be receptive to a recess, a *cooling-off* period. In the interest of an agreement, you may both agree to revisit your parameters and get together again tomorrow, next week, or next month. Although both parties may privately wish there were some way to get back together, they usually don't know how to arrange a reconciliation. Open and honest communication, coupled with an attitude of win-win-win-win, is your key to avoiding an impass.

4. **Impass/Deadlock.** Where communication no longer moves the agreement forward and conversation seems to go in circles. There is nothing wrong with deadlock—either party has the right to prefer no deal to one that falls short of their min-point. How do we break an impass? Change the negotiators, change the parameters, call a third party to mediate, change the shape of money (larger deposit, different terms, cash versus credit), or consider changing venues. These tactics can help

create a climate in which new alternatives can be developed. There is always a way.

5. Agree to Disagree. Both parties may agree to disagree rather than reaching an agreement that compromises both parties, leaving each resentful and disappointed. If your agreement is undermined you may lack the commitment necessary to carry it out. Once again, this could be a temporary situation. Negotiation might be better served two or three months down the road. This tactic can be effective in personal relationships as well. It can even work with your spouse!

6. Confessions. Not only are confessions good for the soul, but they can be a good tactic for negotiators. Confessing—telling all you know, revealing your motives and needs—can be a good way to gain empathy. People tend to be more charitable to someone who tells all. You also demonstrate honesty and a sincere desire to do business. However, no need to share your personal net worth or your most recent sexual fantasy.

Principle #4: Negotiate Price, Don't Sell It

Is price the most important aspect of the sale? No. Never has been, never will be. Customers have never based their buying decisions solely on price and I doubt they ever will. However, salespeople convince themselves that price is the number one motivator to purchase. Studies show that salespeople bring up price before the customer does 60% of the time. Why? I'm not sure but I suppose salespeople feel obligated to bring it up, or perhaps they have been trained to do so. It could even be lack of confidence or corporate self-esteem.

Many salespeople violate the sales process by introducing price too soon. Ideally, price should not be discussed until after your initial confirmation. During the call you need to focus on selling value and benefits to the customer. Don't mention price unless the customer asks or you are negotiating. I realize this concept may seem somewhat manipulative and irresponsible, but it isn't. I have confirmed several deals without the customer or me mentioning price. I think it's part of the rapport and trust issue I spoke of earlier. If a customer trusts you and feels comfortable with you, price is not an important issue. There is an implied understanding that your price will be competitive, otherwise you wouldn't be in business.

By shifting the conversation to price prior to initial confirmation, the salesperson has invited the customer to openly challenge the price. Some salespeople are convinced the customer's mandate is to hammer the salesperson into submission, finally succumbing to a rock-bottom price. Classic tactic of a C account. How to negotiate against price and discount pressure is a common challenge among sales professionals. You've probably heard it before, "Your price is too high. You'll just have to do better," or "It's a competitive market. Your competitors can beat that price," or "You'll have to show more flexibility on your discounting," and so it goes. When salespeople concede too quickly in these situations they not only reduce profitability, but also devalue their customers' perceptions of the product or service. Don't respond by asking, "What's the price they're offering you?" or "What price do I have to beat?" This is a common mistake because it shifts the focus to pure price and discount levels. Experienced negotiators shift the focus to *value* comparisons versus *price* comparisons.

When dealing with the price issue, be guided by knowing your min-max points. If you have price or discount flexibility, do not give it all away at once. Instead, concede slowly and reluctantly. Also, consider trading price concessions for major commitments. It could sound like this: "If I give you X price, will you give me net 10-day terms (or COD terms)?" If the customer is insistent on a discounted price don't hesitate to ask for something from them that makes the deal a win-win-win-win.

Acknowledge the customer's curiosity about price, but don't get sucked into a price debate prior to initial confirmation. For example, when you ask for their business using the five magic words in Chapter 9, your customers may inquire about your price. Simply say, "Yes, I'm sure we both recognize that price is important, but at this point can we agree to do business together based on the benefits discussed, as long as I can give you a competitive price?" If the customer says yes to your *initial* confirmation, you now have a willing party with whom to negotiate. Consider the initial confirmation as a conditional sale; conditional upon working out terms and conditions supported by a competitive price. What salespeople need to realize is that if a fair price cannot be worked out then there is no deal. Final confirmation is conditional upon successful negotiation. However, don't negotiate all aspects of the deal and then focus separately on price. Make sure price or discount is part of the whole package, not a separate negotiation.

During negotiation be cognizant of your customer's behavioral style, and

What an exhausting day. Every time I mentioned price they insisted on a huge discount. This selling stuff is hard work.

adapt. If you are selling to a Director and she wants to know the price prior to *initial* confirmation, I would be inclined to acknowledge the request and offer a price range. Don't be exact with your answer.

Principle #5: Negotiate the Issues, not the Personalities

Often, what causes you to become frustrated or angry in a negotiation is not the topic or issue, but your customer's personality traits. By putting emotional distance between yourself and the negotiation you gain a tremendous advantage. Negotiations often unleash emotions that short-circuit rational processes. We sometimes abandon our carefully designed strategy and resort to a flight or fight response. The key to effective, win-win negotiation is to react unemotionally.

From time to time you may find yourself dealing with an individual you do not particularly care for. Chances are you wouldn't invite him to go camping with you, but he may represent an A account and a sizeable business opportunity. Experienced negotiators understand that professionalism requires the ability to distance oneself from any emotional distractions. These may include biases, perceptions, values, fear of being exploited, egos, feelings, moods, stress, and so on. Parties can get too caught up in the emotions of negotiation. They become *too close* to the deal and overlook important facts that may help move the deal forward. In spite of all your efforts to build a personal relationship you may find yourself dealing with just a corporate relationship. You can both still benefit by simply doing business together and nothing else. Don't entangle relationship challenges within the negotiating process.

For most salespeople, the major barrier is simply the *fear* of negotiation. The very thought sends paralyzing shivers up their spines. The toughest hurdle is learning to be confident enough to stand up to the challenge. This means developing the ability to comfortably express a position without hurting anyone or being hurt. Many people find the straightforward, aggressive, business dialogue of negotiation intimidating. It's the same challenge with confirming: the fear of rejection or perhaps sounding too aggressive. Our natural human tendencies prevail—in our adolescent years we were taught that it was polite not to ask for things and never to be confrontational.

The best approach to dealing with the emotional aspect of negotiation is the pause button. Pushing the pause button means putting the negotiation on hold while you take a break to re-evaluate the situation. This may be for a few minutes or an hour or after you have slept on it. Michael and Mini Donaldson offer this explanation in their book, *Negotiation for Dummies:*

> Knowing when and how to push the pause button not only endows you with an aura of composure and confidence, but also gives you control over all the critical points of the negotiation.

They go on to say:

> No single skill can be as helpful to you as the pause button in any situation laden with heavy emotional overtones. Almost by definition, you cannot fully prepare ahead of time for these situations. Your judicious use of the pause button can compensate. Pushing the pause button produces better results... or at least results that you feel better about.

The message is clear: don't be afraid to utilize your pause button. Use it to re-evaluate your position. Perhaps in the interest of flexibility it can become an opportunity to reconsider your must-have issues and your min-max points. Remember, with two willing parties, there is always a way.

Law of 10 Options

A few years ago I had the pleasure of hearing Jim Rohn, an international motivational speaker, speak at a sales conference in Calgary. One of his many suggestions was to be guided in life, and in sales, by the Law of Ten Options. His point is this: with a cancellation or postponement of an event, there are always ten other options—ten alternatives to consider. For example: if you and your spouse had planned an evening out with the Jones but at the last minute they gracefully declined due to sickness, you now have ten options to consider—go see a movie, see a play, visit other friends, clean the garage, read a book and so on. All is not lost because of a sudden change in plans. The first five or six options may present themselves quite readily, whereas the final three or four may require some creative thinking—perhaps even some alternatives outside your comfort zone. It works well. My wife and I often discuss our ten options and frequently come up with options that are as enjoyable or more enjoyable than the original cancelled event.

Rohn's law can be applied to all situations and it can be particularly useful in pursuing the spirit of creative negotiation. Have some fun with it. Anyone with teenagers will immediately understand how effective it can be—teenagers exercise the Law of Ten Options on a daily basis.

Negotiation is not a game with a single objective but rather one step in building effective long-term relationships. It is only one of the ten steps in your Sequential Model but it can be the pivotal point in your relationship and your success. During negotiation you forge an agreement—like taking the relationship from a courtship to a marriage. "Will you marry me?" may not be your actual request but your final confirmation (the five magic words) certainly suggests the commitment and responsibilities of a marriage.

One of the surest ways to successful negotiation is to be well prepared. It's essential, but planning is often overlooked in the excitement of approaching the finish line. It's like training and conditioning to run a marathon but then running out of steam at the 24-mile mark. So many salespeople come close to the finish line but fail to complete the race because of a lack of training and preparation. We cannot afford to ignore the dire consequences of inadequate preparation. Planning is not an isolated step of your Sequential Model but is a prerequisite to successful graduation of each and every step—including creative negotiation.

The skills outlined in this chapter will help you to build confidence and reach your business and personal objectives. Understand not only how to negotiate, but when. Review the five principles regularly and continue to fuel your confidence to not only run a good marathon, but to finish it.

NOTES

1. Achievers International. Creative Negotiations Workshop. 1989.

Congratulations, you have now completed
Step #8

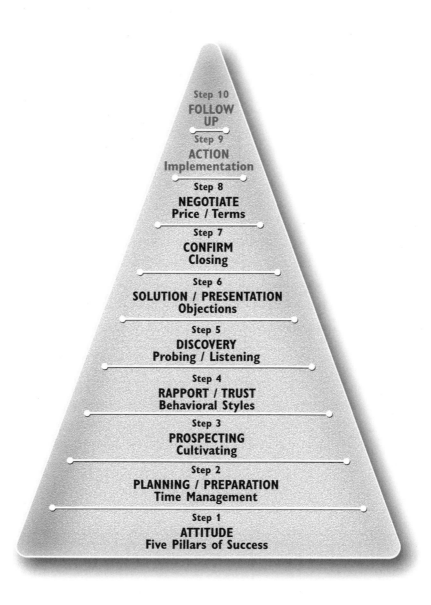

Step 10
FOLLOW
UP

Step 9
ACTION
Implementation

Step 8
NEGOTIATE
Price / Terms

Step 7
CONFIRM
Closing

Step 6
SOLUTION / PRESENTATION
Objections

Step 5
DISCOVERY
Probing / Listening

Step 4
RAPPORT / TRUST
Behavioral Styles

Step 3
PROSPECTING
Cultivating

Step 2
PLANNING / PREPARATION
Time Management

Step 1
ATTITUDE
Five Pillars of Success

Chapter 11

ACTION PLAN: IMPLEMENTATION

Congratulations on your successful negotiation. The customer said yes, you reached a win-win-win-win agreement, and now it's time to take action. This is what you have been working so hard to achieve, the opportunity to showcase your company and your product, and to deliver on all the benefits and promises you presented earlier. However, in many ways, your job is just beginning. Just as in a marriage the, "I do" should be, "I will do." Your customers have high expectations—don't let them down. In fact, the more they spend, the higher their expectations. People expect their purchases to be perfect and hassle-free.

Surprisingly, the details of an effective action plan are often overlooked in the euphoria of finally anchoring the deal. Nevertheless, your role now is to quarterback all the activities necessary for a smooth, seamless implementation rather than race to the car, dig out a calculator and excitedly work out your commission and/or bonus. It's important that you identify and delegate responsibilities to ensure a timely, hassle-free delivery of your solution. A big part of what your customer just purchased is peace of mind about a worry-free delivery. Customers need to feel they have made a wise, intelligent investment. Initially they may feel a little uneasy, insecure about their decision. After all, you have convinced them to embrace change.

My People Need to Talk to Your People

All parties must understand their roles and responsibilities and work in harmony for a smooth implementation. It's a good idea for both you and your customer to identify all parties involved in the implementation: "This is what I'll do, within this time frame, and these are the people to involve." Parties involved may include management, operations, accounting, manufacturing, engineering, shipping/receiving, inventory control, technical people, delivery people, and so on. You can't do it alone, so draw on the strengths of your internal customers and your customer's people to ensure a smooth, speedy, hassle-free implementation. With all parties working in harmony, the story of these four people becomes a reality:[1]

WHAT WENT RIGHT?

This is the story of four people: *Everybody, Anybody, Somebody,* and *Nobody.* There was an important job to be done and *Nobody* was sure that *Anybody* would do it but instead *Somebody* did it. *Nobody* got angry because it was *Anybody's* job. There was no need for *Nobody* to blame *Anybody*—*Somebody* did the job *Anybody* could have done. *Nobody* made excuses but *Everybody* was satisfied.

Communication at the best of times is fraught with uncertainty, biases, and individual perceptions. Effective communication is a topic onto its own. Poor communication often results in costly oversights and mistakes. Communication is a very delicate, fragile process. As responsible sales entrepreneurs, we need to ensure an effective exchange of information.

For larger, more sophisticated deals, I suggest both parties safeguard themselves against the normal pitfalls of communication and consider drafting a letter of intent or a letter of agreement. I don't mean a legal document that requires hiring a lawyer at $50 for every three minutes, I simply mean putting a letter together on your company letterhead outlining the logistics of the deal. Who is doing what and by when? You and your customer can review it for accuracy and completeness, signing your respective copies.

Part of your responsibilities also include avoiding, or at least minimizing, user error. To do so you must evaluate your customer's abilities, technical or otherwise, and recommend training if necessary. Research suggests that up to 30% of the time customers are *wrong*. Reported product and service problems resulted from customer error, product misuse, or failure to read the instructions. Customers do screw up, but as professionals we have to allow them to maintain dignity. It takes a strong *attitude* to let certain things go while biting your tongue. You must also make your customer aware of the break-in period, the time required to fully appreciate the benefits of your product or service. This may not be apparent initially. True happiness will only come once everyone is using your product correctly.

Tim Commandment #8
Create an action plan.
Ask: What are my implementation strategies?

Customers Don't Shoot the Messenger

We no longer live in times where they behead the messenger, although I'm sure that on occasions customers are tempted. In the eyes of customers, the salesperson is ultimately responsible for seeing that the product or service is delivered when promised. If problems arise when filling an order (and this is not unusual), customers should be informed promptly. The progress of the order or any possible back orders should also be monitored and communicated to the customer so that if something goes wrong alternative arrangements can be made. Customers may not jump for joy at the news, but they will certainly appreciate the opportunity to take corrective action.

Customers can become disgruntled for a number of reasons, most of which turn out to be minor when handled properly, tactfully, and in a timely manner. Dealing with panic-stricken customers demanding instant satisfaction can be an emotionally draining exercise. These intolerable nuisances, if left unresolved, can easily and quickly escalate into a mountainous catastrophe. Unfortunately, human beings tend to focus on the negative—what went wrong versus what went right. Your phone call will go a long way to prevent the proverbial poop from hitting the fan. Be the bearer of bad news before your customers call you. When *you* call they will be easier to manage, but when *they* call it's too late—they're in no mood to listen to your blamefest.

Monitoring order processing and other after-sales activity is critical to developing a partnership. A *Purchasing Magazine* study indicated that failure to follow through after the sale was the second-biggest complaint of buyers. What was the first one? Talking too much.

Many specific activities are essential to ensure customer loyalty and satisfaction. Sales entrepreneurs must be jugglers. Continue to build trust, monitor proper usage, assist in servicing the account, and provide expert guidance and assistance. Adopting an empathetic attitude to a real or imaginary problem cannot be overemphasized.

NOTES

1. Achievers International. Situational Selling Workshop. 1989.

Congratulations, you have now completed Step #9

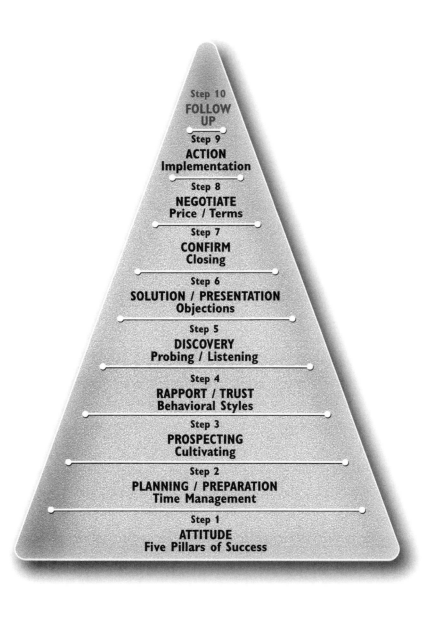

Step 10
FOLLOW UP

Step 9
ACTION
Implementation

Step 8
NEGOTIATE
Price / Terms

Step 7
CONFIRM
Closing

Step 6
SOLUTION / PRESENTATION
Objections

Step 5
DISCOVERY
Probing / Listening

Step 4
RAPPORT / TRUST
Behavioral Styles

Step 3
PROSPECTING
Cultivating

Step 2
PLANNING / PREPARATION
Time Management

Step 1
ATTITUDE
Five Pillars of Success

Chapter 12

FOLLOW-UP: YOU NEVER CALL OR WRITE ANYMORE

Have you ever heard that line? I have. Your parents and friends sometimes say it to you, but your customers have a different way of saying it. Customers complain with their feet; they walk. If a customer ever says it or suggests it, you had better pay attention. It could be the death knell for your relationship.

Effective follow-up after confirmation and successful negotiation means going that little bit extra for your customer. The little things often move a relationship forward. The result is a win-win-win-win. The win for you is anchoring a solid client, a source of referrals, and second-selling opportunities within an existing account. When we treat our customers with respect and appreciation we feel good about ourselves. At the same time, our customers feel good about working with us. A long-term business relationship is forged.

It's a fact that customers will forget you within 27 days. Your parents might even forget you every couple of months. You have worked hard through Steps #1 to #9 and now it's time to use all your resources and tools to protect your newly acquired asset. You must build a fortress of loyalty to keep the watchful eye of your competitors out. I have often said that getting the first sale is easy. It's getting the repeat orders that truly validates your performance as a sales entrepreneur.

Keeping your customer happy and satisfied requires conscious effort. It is part of the ongoing process of assessment, feedback, and reassessment that makes you continually responsive to your customer. It's difficult to coordinate the pursuit of new customers while servicing and growing existing accounts. I think this anonymous quote says it well: "A relationship will deteriorate over time. A natural tendency of any relationship (business or marriage) is toward erosion of sensitivity and attentiveness. It requires a solid effort against the forces of decline." A powerful statement indeed.

Too often we take our good customers (As and Bs) for granted. They are the ones who are easy to deal with, rarely giving us trouble. They even provide positive word-of-mouth, recommending our product or service to associates and friends. Because they give us little trouble and are low-maintenance, we often forget about them. "Out of sight, out of mind." Sales entrepreneurs realize the adage: "Business goes to those who want it and work hard for it, and stays with those who work even harder and show appreciation for it." You must guard against complacency and overconfidence. Don't become vulnerable to your competition.

Here's something I bet you haven't even thought about, much less analyzed. What is your customer *attrition* rate? Surprisingly, most businesses experience a 10–30% attrition rate, but few salespeople are aware of the impact customer erosion has on a business. Unfortunately, experience tells us that the "customer for life" concept is only a myth. Customers are only for a measurable period of time. The goal is to build loyalty to have (and to hold) as much of the customer's attention as realistically possible, for as long as possible. Buyers are selective today and can be frighteningly fickle. The fact is that by not appreciating or expressing gratitude for their business, 10–30% of your customers will leave or at least reduce the frequency of business they do with you. Ironically, you probably wrestle with, "Where do I find new business?" Yet the easiest and most inexpensive method is not to lose them in the first place.

Price is rarely, if ever, the culprit for high attrition. In the majority of situations, it is an attitude of indifference that drives customers away, motivated by a competitor who is more than happy to shower them with lots of attention during the courting phase. Your customers want to feel that they are appreciated and valued by you, not merely seen as a dollar transaction. I'm not suggesting you can ever eliminate attrition, but you can proactively minimize its debilitating effect on the growth of your business.

> *Just as little things can turn a customer off, little things*
> *will turn a customer on.*

Protecting your customer base is a top priority. It's the difference between selling hard or selling smart. Research tells us that it's five to six times more expensive to replace a customer than to keep one. I suppose it's no different than divorce. So, how do you show your customers that you think of them often and that you love 'em? In a relationship there is only one way to say, "I love you," but there are countless ways of showing it. Speaking for my gender, males are known for not communicat-

ing feelings or expressing emotions. In relationships, we don't
tell our spouse or significant other, "I love you" often enough.
The response is more like this; "Honey, you know I love you and
if that changes, you'll be the second to know." Your mate appre-
ciates hearing, "I love you," just as your customers need to hear
and see your appreciation for their business.

Ten Follow-Up Letters

Don't underestimate the power of the humble thank-you note.
Thank-you notes clearly indicate to the recipients that you've
made an effort to think about them and thank them for their
support. Consider the last time you received a handwritten invitation or note of thanks. Feels good, doesn't it? You can use
thank-you notes for a variety of occasions. They confirm your
commitment and help solidify your business relationship,
making it more difficult for your competitors to replace you.
Use handwritten notes for just about any situation or occasion.
I offer you these ten suggestions for follow-up notes. Feel free
to modify or tailor these notes to your specific situation. I offer
these as guidelines only.

1. **After a purchase.** Thank you for giving me the opportunity of providing you with the benefits of our product. I am
confident that you will be happy with your investment and I
will endeavor to offer excellent follow-up service. I do appreciate your support.

2. **A first meeting.** Thank you for taking the time to
meet with me. I enjoyed our visit and the opportunity to learn
more about your business. I look forward to our next meeting.

3. **Telephone contact.** Thank you for taking the time to
chat with me on the telephone. You'll soon receive all the information we discussed. I look forward to following up with you

next week to discuss the details of our proposal and the possibility of a win-win agreement.

4. After a presentation/demonstration. Thank you for the opportunity to showcase our products and services to you (and to your committee). My presentation highlighted the key benefits of our product and outlined the mutual benefits of an association of our firms. I look forward to our follow-up meeting next Wednesday at 2:30 PM. See you then.

5. A turndown or they buy from someone else. Thank you for taking the time to analyze my proposal. I regret being unable, at this time, to demonstrate our capabilities. However, we are constantly responding to our customers' expectations and to new trends, developments, and changes in our industry. Thus, I will keep in touch with the hope that in the near future we will be able to do business.

This classy tactic clearly shows your professionalism and encourages the customer to seriously consider you for *next time.* A great tactic to become #2.

6. A gatekeeper. Thank you for providing me with the opportunity to meet with Mr. Smith. Our meeting was productive and there may be an opportunity for our companies to do business. I will let you know how things work out.

7. A referral. Thank you for the valuable referral. I look forward to meeting with Ms. Jones. You can rest assured that I will exercise the same level of professionalism that I have with you. I will let you know how things work out.

8. A turndown but they offer to give a referral. Thank you for your generous offer to provide me with a referral. I am saddened to hear your immediate plans do not include us but I will keep you posted on new services that may benefit you.

9. **An anniversary.** Thank you. It's with pleasure that I send this note on the one-year anniversary of your patronage. Your support is appreciated—clients like you contribute to our success. I have enclosed an update on our latest advancements and I'll give you a call next week to discuss them further.

10. **A cold call.** Thank you for making the time to chat with me when I visited your office recently. I learned a great deal about your business needs and expectations. I look forward to following up with your people next week. I'll stay in touch.

Follow these six suggestions to maximize the impact of your note:

1. **Handwritten.** Personalize it with your own handwriting. If your penmanship is sloppy, write slower.

2. **Don't use company letterhead.** Buy some nice stationary that doesn't scream "business letter." It must be a personal gesture.

3. **Handwrite the envelope too.** Personalize the whole package.

4. **Buy stamps.** Use a stamp. Don't put it through a mailing machine. A typed envelope with a corporate stamp on it takes away from the personal touch. It also looks lazy.

5. **Include your business card.** It clearly indicates who this note is from. A handwritten note simply signed by you may cause confusion or uncertainty as to the sender. Your customer may not know you all that well—yet.

6. **Don't expect a response.** Although it may seem your efforts have gone unnoticed, your customers do appreciate it. In these busy times, customers simply don't have time to pick up

the phone and thank you. I once sent a note and heard nothing back but the next time I made a call my note was displayed on her credenza.

Tim Commandment #9
Business will stay where it's appreciated. Ask: How have I demonstrated my appreciation?

I Still Love You

How many ways are there to express your appreciation and show your customers you love 'em? That's up to you. Just as Paul Simon suggested that there are "50 ways to leave your lover," there are countless ways to show your sincerity to the relationship. Let's consider a few: a simple phone call, a note on their invoice or delivery box, a delivery of balloons, cookies, chocolates, a fruit basket, a lottery ticket, a corporate treat (logo'ed pens, hats, shirts, note pads, golf balls, etc.) a gift certificate for two at an upscale restaurant, a copy of this book, (yes, that was a pitch, I couldn't resist!) or any other publication or magazine, tickets to a sporting or community event, the list goes on. Highlight any that may have triggered some ideas to pursue with your customers. "We love you and appreciate your business" should show in your every deed, because business usually stays where it's appreciated.

Give us a call or e-mail me at tim@spectrain.com with any unique, off the wall, follow-up tactics that have worked for you. For sharing your ideas, I'll send *you* a treat. The bottom line is, follow-up is the essence to any successful relationship.

Congratulations, you have now completed
Step #10

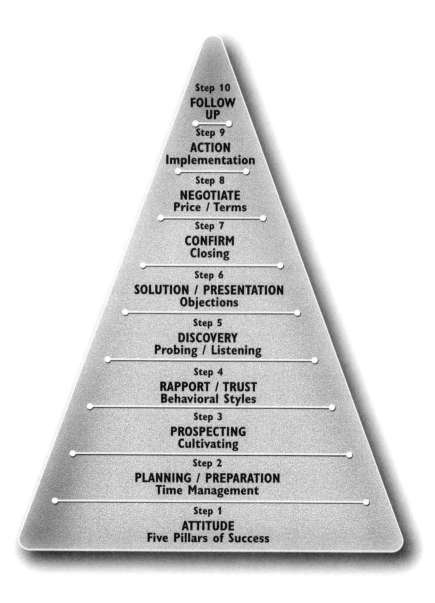

CONCLUSION

Congratulations. You've covered a lot of material, and have successfully graduated through all ten steps of your Sequential Model. Welcome to this year's graduating class of sales entrepreneurs. You are now part of an elite group of professionals.

Now the fun begins. Application of the strategies and techniques throughout the Sequential Model enables you to navigate with confidence through the entire sales call, steadily moving your customer toward a buying decision. Your completed Sequential Model is a continuous loop guiding you through every aspect of the relationship, with each completed step setting up the next. Your biggest challenge now will be to unlearn cherished old sales habits and to embrace the new techniques outlined throughout the Sequential Model.

Change is a prerequisite to success. Learning is a sequential process marked by stages of growth and development. Learning is cumulative. Practice is the key.

A central theme throughout the book focuses on the role and responsibilities of sales entrepreneurs. Sales organizations are slowly reshaping themselves to foster entrepreneurial approaches to selling. You are no longer expected to be servicing a territory, but managing a business. The future will not be an option for sales representatives—they need not apply.

I share with you a comment from a very successful sales entrepreneur: "You beat 50% of the salespeople in North America just by working hard. You beat another 40% by being a person of honesty and integrity. The last 10% is a dogfight in the free enterprise system." I agree. His comment is a strong reminder of the importance of embracing an entrepreneurial code of conduct, guided by your Sequential Model.

Earlier in the book I discussed the importance of a winning edge and the compelling influence that attitude has on your personal life and your career. The importance of the five attitudinal pillars and how they are intrinsically linked to success cannot be underestimated. Attitude drives skills. Without it all other skills are handicapped. Attitude is a powerful differentiator in a world of fierce competition riddled with "pick me, pick me" competitors.

One of the emerging challenges of our times is not about price or product performance—it's about providing after-sales service that exceeds the expected, that delivers the 1% Solution. Use effective implementation and follow-up strategies to minimize your customer attrition rate. Complacency is the most common thief of good customers. Let them know frequently that you think of them and you still love 'em.

Again, congratulations on a successful journey through your Sequential Model. I leave you with three powerful words: JUST DID IT

P.S. I would love to know how these strategies are helping you. Send me your success stories at: tim@spectrain.com or fax me at (403)269–3483.

Thank you.

Tim Commandment #10
Celebrate and reward yourself.
Ask: What went right?

BIBLIOGRAPHY

Alessandra, Tony and O'Connor, Michael. *People Smarts.* (San Diego: Pfeiffer and Company, 1994).

Alessandra, Tony and O'Connor, Michael J. *The Platinum Rule.* (New York: Warner Books Inc., 1996).

Boyan, Lee. *Successful Cold Call Selling.* (New York: American Management Association, 1989).

Carlson, Richard. *Don't Sweat The Small Stuff...and it's all small stuff.* (New York: Hyperion, 1997).

Carnegie, Dale. *How To Win Friends & Influence People.* Carnegie, Dale (New York: Simon & Schuster Inc., 1981).

Chilton, David. *The Wealthy Barber.* (Toronto: Stoddart Publishing Co. Limited, 1989).

Chapman, Elwood N. *Life Is An Attitude!* (Menlo Park: Crisp Publications, Inc., 1992).

Creative Negotiation. Achievers International (1989).

Donaldson, Michael and Mimi. *Negotiating for Dummies.* (Foster City: IDG Books Worldwide, Inc., 1996).

Nelson, Bob and Economy, Peter. *Managing for Dummies.* (Foster City: IDG Books Worldwide, Inc., 1996).

Situational Selling: Focus on the Customer. Achievers International (1989).

Tieger, Paul and Barbara. *The Art of Speedreading People.* (Little Brown, 1998).

Wilson, Larry. *Changing the Game: The New Way to Sell.* (New York: Simon & Schuster Inc., 1987).

RECOMMENDED READINGS

Alessandra, Tony and O'Connor, Michael J. *The Platinum Rule.*

Bolton, Robert and Grover, Dorothy. *People Styles at Work.*

Boyan, Lee. *Successful Cold Call Selling.*

Canfield, Jack and Hansen, Mark Victor and Hewitt, Les. *The Power of Focus.*

Carlson, Richard. *Don't Sweat The Small Stuff...and it's all small stuff.*

Carnegie, Dale. *How to Win Friends & Influence People.*

Chapman, Elwood N. *Life Is an Attitude!*

Chilton, David. *The Wealthy Barber.*

Cloke, Kenneth and Goldsmith, Joan. *Thank God It's Monday!*

Covey, Stephen. *The 7 Habits of Highly Effective People.*

Frankl, Viktor E. *Man's Search for Meaning.*

Hill, Napoleon. *Think & Grow Rich.*

Nelson, Bob. *1001 Ways to Reward Employees.*

Reeve, Christopher. *Still Me.*

Sharma, Robin. *The Monk Who Sold His Ferrari.*

INDEX